To: _____

From: _____

Thank you, beloved, for your support. May the God of Restoration restore unto you everything that you have lost or was stolen from you. I wish you and your family continued success.

Jasmine Gordon

Daily Restorational
52-Weeks of Devotion

It's Time to Restore Everything Held Captive or Stolen From You.

Jasmine Gordon
Servant

Copyright © 2021 Nichole "Jasmine" Gordon
ISBN 978-1-7353091-6-3

All Rights Reserved

All Rights Reserved. No part of this book may be reproduced or transmitted in any form or by any means, electronically or mechanically, including photocopying, recording, or by an information storage and retrieval system without permission in writing from the author of this book.

Scriptures marked (KJV) are taken from the KING JAMES VERSION (KJV): KING JAMES VERSION, public domain.

Scripture quotations marked (NIV) are taken from THE HOLY BIBLE, NEW INTERNATIONAL VERSION®, NIV® Copyright © 1973, 1978, 1984, 2011 by Biblica, Inc.™ Used by permission. All rights reserved worldwide.

Scripture quotations marked (NLT) are taken from the Holy Bible, New Living Translation, copyright © 1996, 2004, 2007 by Tyndale House Foundation. Used by permission of Tyndale House Publishers, Inc., Carol Stream, IL 60188. All rights reserved.

Scripture quotations marked (ESV) are taken from The Holy Bible, English Standard Version® (ESV®), copyright © 2001 by Crossway, a publishing ministry of Good News Publishers. Used by permission. All rights reserved.

Scripture quotations marked (AMP) are taken from Copyright (c) 1954, 1958, 1962, 1964, 1965, 1987 by The Lockman Foundation, La Habra, CA 90631All rights reserved. https://www.lockman.org.

Scripture quotations marked (GWT) are taken from GOD'S WORD is a copyrighted work of God's Word to the Nations. Quotations are used by permission. Copyright 1995 by God's Word to the Nations. All rights reserved.

Editor:
Shawna E. Brown

Proofreader:
Ruby Porter

Published by:

DOMINIONHOUSE
Publishing & Design, LLC
P.O. Box 681938 | Orlando, Florida 32868 | 407.703.4800
www.mydominionhouse.com

*****

Author Contact:

www.mwbint.org
Email: mwb8870@gmail.com
718.781.0521 | 804.720.6080

Dedication

This devotional is dedicated to those who have suffered loss, humiliation, betrayal, intimidation, fear, and countless other atrocities. It is dedicated to those who struggle with their inner selves, feelings of inferiority or low self-esteem and to those who lack knowledge regarding spiritual warfare.

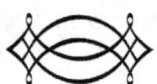

"God is preparing to restore your soul and lead you in the paths of righteousness, abundance, and favor. Let go and let Him."

Epigraph

If you have SALVATION on a layaway plan,
it's time to pick it up. It's paid for, in full.

-Jasmine Gordon

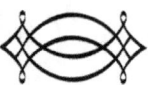

I will restore the fortunes of my people Israel, and they shall rebuild the ruined cities and inhabit them; they shall plant vineyards and drink their wine, and they shall make gardens and eat their fruit.

Amos 9:14 ESV

Table of Restorational

Foreword 15

Introduction 19

Week 1
Restore My Faith 25

Week 2
Restore My Appreciation 30

Week 3
Restore My Integrity 34

Week 4
Restore My Self-Worth 38

Week 5
Restore My Identity 42

Week 6
Restore My Character 46

Week 7
Restore My Conscience 50

Week 8
Restore My Boldness 54

Week 9
Restore My Discipline 60

Week 10
Restore My Humility 65

Week 11
Restore My Will-Power 69

Table of Restorational

Week 12
Restore My Self-Control................73

Week 13
Restore My Health/Memory 77

Week 14
Restore My Strength...................81

Week 15
Restore My Years.....................85

Week 16
Restore My Marriage..................89

Week 17
Restore My Family....................94

Week 18
Restore My Relationship...............99

Week 19
Restore My Child's/Children's Mind 104

Week 20
Restore My Prayer Life................109

Week 21
Restore My Salvation.................114

Week 22
Restore My Fear of God...............121

Week 23
Restore My Anointing.................125

Table of Restorational

Week 24
Restore My Discernment 130

Week 25
Restore My Excellence 134

Week 26
Restore My Servant's Heart 140

Week 27
Restore My Obedience 144

Week 28
Restore My Gratitude 149

Week 29
Restore My Patience 153

Week 30
Restore My Wisdom 158

Week 31
Restore My Compassion 162

Week 32
Restore My Voice 167

Week 33
Restore My Favor 172

Week 34
Restore My Knowledge of Revelation 176

Week 35
Restore My Finances 181

Table of Restorational

Week 36
Restore My Possession 187

Week 37
Restore My Community 195

Week 38
Restore My Church .201

Week 39
Restore My Hearing .206

Week 40
Restore My Fasting .212

Week 41
Restore My Commitment 216

Week 42
Restore My Consistency 221

Week 43
Restore My Focus 225

Week 44
Restore My Zeal 230

Week 45
Restore My Respect 234

Week 46
Restore My Peace 238

Week 47
Restore My Joy 243

Table of Restorational

Week 48
Restore My Hope 247

Week 49
Restore My Trust 252

Week 50
Restore My Worship 257

Week 51
Restore My Praise 261

Week 52
Restore My Confidence 266

A Call to Salvation 270

Repentance Prayer 272

Closing Prayer
A Prayer Just For You .273

Appendix

Names of God – El 277

Names of God – Jehovah 279

Note of Thanks 281

References 282

About the Author 283

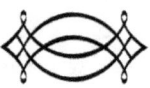

This is your hour of restoration. God is getting ready to RESTORE unto you everything that was broken, stolen, destroyed, held in bondage, or captivity. Be open to receive divine restoration.

Foreword

Apparently, a book can make you or destroy you. I recall a time when I attended an important interview for my career. The building where the interview was held was one of the most beautiful and prominent skyscrapers in Manhattan, New York. To the interview, I took my blueprint portfolio, which was at least 30 pages long. It was from a Computer-Aided Design (CAD) internship that I had previously finished. I remember feeling excited, confident, and over-zealous as I entered, I thought that it was one of the most fascinating buildings in the city to meet the interviewer for my undergraduate studies program at the Massachusetts Institute of Technology (MIT).

The interviewer looked like a young man in his late thirties who seemed very accomplished. I still remember his disorganized office space, which was a dry and rustic atmosphere with books and items strewn everywhere. We sat across from each other in his office, and he immediately began testing me. His voice was frosty, never cordial, and he rigorously tested my knowledge of arithmetic, statistics, and logic. After an hour of questioning, he surmised that I was competent enough to answer each of his questions. He then looked at me and sternly asked, "Have you read, *Look Homeward, Angel?*" With disappointment, I replied "No, I have not." He continued, "You have not heard of or read *Look Homeward, Angel* by Thomas Wolfe?" I replied, "Well, I have read several great kinds of literature, just not that one." The interview ended with a bitter argument between him and myself regarding why I believed familiarity with one book should not determine a person's knowledge of literature and admission to a university. Before going home that day, I went to the Barnes and Noble bookstore to purchase the book mentioned. I took only three days to read it in its entirety. Somehow, I felt like my unsuccessful college interview was a direct result of not having read that one book, which I have, subsequently, regretted. I was denied admission to college because I failed to read the one book my interviewer strongly believed was revolutionary.

Similar to my aforementioned interviewer, I expressly recommend to you the one book I believe will cause a turning point in your life; *Daily Restorational* by Jasmine Gordon. I first met the author, Evangelist Jasmine Gordon, at a prayer summit where we were both invited as guest speakers. The fellowship during that hour and the impression that she made on me through her illustrative sermon has since lingered with me as a most fragrant memory. As an intercessor and the Director of *Prayer Cell International*, I have read an immense amount of literature regarding the subject of prayer. Still, few books on the subject are as intimate and transforming as Evangelist Gordon's devotional entitled, *Daily Restorational*.

Evangelist Gordon does not teach us to pray in this devotional nor does she focus on the technicalities and the dynamics of the art of prayer. Instead, in this book, she emphasizes that one must learn to pray by praying. She has invited the reader into her prayer closet to join in the fellowship of pure, non-mechanical, and transforming prayer.

This devotional is so timely! Indeed, in such a time as this, we need to cry out for restoration. I am privileged to give the clarion invitation to enter the prayer closet with Evangelist Gordon and allow this *Daily Restorational* devotion book to ignite the fire of your prayer life. I invite you to pray and command restoration in your physical and spiritual lives, because prayer works when all other efforts fail. Prayer can do all things, and it turns the Hand which turns the world. Given what can be accomplished with prayer, why do it using your own strength? Save your energy. What you can combat with prayer, you could never overcome using your own hands, so save your power. Much can be acquired through prayer, more than what you could, otherwise, face alone. Do not toil all night in carnality.

Evangelist Jasmine Gordon has simplified the closet talk in *Daily Restorational*. I believe this book will enhance your walk with God. Remember, sometimes all it takes is one book to make an entire world of difference in your life. I highly recommend this book, to allow prayer to be the vehicle which molds you into who God desires you to be.

Cephas K. Agbesi
Honeywell Baptist Church, New York (Senior Pastor)
Powerpoint Worship Center, New Jersey (Senior Pastor)
Prayer Cell International (Director)

Behold, I will do a new thing, Now it shall spring forth; Shall you not know it? I will even make a road in the wilderness And rivers in the desert.

Isaiah 43:19

Introduction

Daily Restorational? Yes. It was strongly impressed in my spirit to name this book *Daily Restorational* instead of Daily Devotional. I am fully aware that *"Retorational"* is not a word, at least not yet. Ultimately, it is all about asking God to restore everything we lose, on a daily basis. *Daily Restorational* will open our eyes and bring awareness to the many unused and unidentified weapons that we have in our arsenal. As you read along, you will learn about the various weapons and how to use them.

Ironically, this *Daily Restorational* is being completed during a time when everyone is seeking restoration as a result of the unexpected, world-wide Coronavirus pandemic, also referred to as COVID-19, in the year 2020. I began writing this restorational simultaneously with my other book titled, *38 Reasons for Unanswered Prayers* in October of 2013, immediately after publishing my first book, Fear Not! There Is Still Power In Prayer. Even though half of *Daily Restorational* was professionally edited in 2014, it was a struggle to complete the remaining chapters. I faced one delay after another, including intense writer's block as well as personal obstacles. Now, I understand why I could not finish writing this book the first time; the final chapter was not yet created. WOW! With the book still in my possession, I was able to edit, insert, and delete components of the text as more insight was gathered. It is amazing how God allows things to fall into place, not according to our time but in His time. As the saying goes, "Nothing is done before its time."

We are living in a somber time; a time of uncertainty and danger, while experiencing many social and spiritual calamities. Worldwide, men are scrambling to find themselves, their purpose, and answers to many mysteries, including the COVID-19 pandemic. With continuing and complex difficulties arising, it is challenging to manage the many things around us which appear to be falling apart, and it is hard to grasp the rapid changes. People feel unstable, and many have lost their will to live, the joy to celebrate, the desire to be among people, and the interest to pursue their dreams. Some people may have willfully given up and relinquished their power and sense of self. Nonetheless, it is time to restore all that has been lost. The word *restore* means to bring back or return something that was lost or stolen from you; to *replace, reinstate; replenish* or *re-establish* again into your possession.

This fifty-two week, *Daily Restorational* was written and published to help you start your day on the right path. The primary intent of this restorational is to heighten your awareness without being ignorant of the ways Satan fights and the devices, tactics, and weapons he uses. It will also teach you how to fight back, victoriously. Satan doesn't mind if you remain ignorant of his cunning actions or his strategies to destroy your future, nor does he mind you blaming someone or something else for the havoc he is wreaking in your life. Many people do not believe in spiritual warfare so they suffer, unnecessarily, at the hand of Satan and his agents. Some individuals may argue and question why every adverse situation has to be associated with the devil. They may also say we give too much credit to Satan and his demons.

Many people suffer from various kinds of illnesses, sleepless nights, one disappointment after the next, strange life experiences, and weird occurrences happening to their family members or at their job. However, they still believe these happenings are normal and they do nothing to respond to them. Consider your nightly dreams. What have you been dreaming about? Pay closer attention, and start writing down the details of your dreams. God still speaks to His people through dreams and visions. If there is a God, there is a devil. If there is Heaven, there is a Hell. And if there is good, there is certainly evil.

Introduction

Revelation 12:12^{KJV} reads, Therefore rejoice, ye heavens, and ye that dwell in them. Woe to the inhabiters of the earth and of the sea! For the devil is come down unto you, having great wrath, because he knoweth that he hath but a short time.

2 Corinthians 2:11^{KJV} reads, Lest Satan should get an advantage of us: for we are not ignorant of his devices.

You may have noticed that–restorational is unlike typical devotionals. It is structured to provide in-depth information for you to ponder throughout the week and to consider for a lifetime. You will be enlightened regarding multiple strategies the enemy uses to impede your success; and you will be taught how to fight against those intrusions and restore your growth. Most importantly, you will identify things you may have, purposely, surrendered to the enemy. Each week, you are encouraged to read and pray using a specific chapter for seven days at a time. You will learn how to take back from the enemy what is rightfully yours, recite warfare prayers against Satan and his cohorts, as well as pray God's promises over your life. The prayers are intentionally personalized so you can pray these words according to your circumstances. However, some of the topics may not, directly, apply to your situation, so feel free to improvise. Also, you may not recognize some of the names mentioned to address God; but they are all used in relation to scriptural references. For example, God is referred to as more than Jehovah Jireh, Jehovah Rapha, Jehovah Shalom, and other familiar names with which you may already be familiar.

The prayers in this book are to be prayed, not just read. They are, strategically, written to assist those who believe, but say they cannot pray or don't know how to pray. Whenever you approach God during prayer, you must first:

Acknowledge - Acknowledge the Lord for who He is while offering praise or adoration.

Confess - Confess your sins to Jesus Christ; and ask for forgiveness, which is repentance or confession.

Thanksgiving - Give God thanks for His forgiveness, goodness, and mercy towards you.

Supplication - Ask God to intervene in your situation; and request your heart's desire through supplication or petitions.

Some refer to this method as the A.C.T.S. or P.R.A.Y. method. Don't forget to yield or linger, quietly, in God's presence after praying; as you listen for His response or direction. The prayers in this *Daily Restorational* are formatted using the A.C.T.S. method with one slight difference; offering thanksgiving is saved for the end of the prayers.

P = Praise	A = Adoration
R = Repent	C = Confession
A = Ask	T = Thanksgiving
Y = Yield	S = Supplication

Somewhere, along life's journey, we may have lost our sense of direction because of the many afflictions we suffered. We were used, abused, and refused numerous times by the people we claim to love. We have been robbed of our innocence, our sense of self, and our rights; and we remain unsettled. Negativity often breeds negativity! If we are not careful, negative thoughts can send our minds spiraling out of control, which cause us to question our self-worth. We interrogate ourselves with questions, such as:

Introduction

Why am I here?

Will I ever be somebody?

Will I ever be able to fulfill my purpose and reach my destiny?

Will I ever be loved or be happy? Can my circumstances change for the better?

Will I ever regain my health? How do I know when it's my season?

Will I ever be accepted?

The list continues! If the enemy of our mind can convince us to anticipate negative answers to these questions, then he has met his goal to keep us in perpetual negativity.

Some of us have suffered tremendous loss and have never fully recovered from the grief. Given the magnitude of the loss, many people reach their breaking points and may experience thoughts of suicide. Some may feel overwhelmed with their situations and see no hope in sight. Even though *Daily Restorational* can be read any time of the day, I firmly believe if you start your daily routine with this book, it will provide the foundation for clarity throughout your day. With this base, questions will be answered, granting you progress towards restoration in your life. My friend, do not quit! Your moment of restoration is likely closer than you can imagine. Therefore, open your mouth and declare, "I AM RESTORED!"

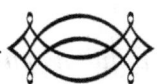

I believe faith is the vehicle that will transport and transform your dreams into reality and make your unseen promises tangible. Restore your faith in God.

_____ *Week 1*

•••
Restore My Faith

Jesus answered and said unto them, Verily I say unto you, If ye have faith, and doubt not, ye shall not only do this which is done to the fig tree, but also if ye shall say unto this mountain, Be thou removed, and be thou cast into the sea; it shall be done. Matthew 21:21^{KJV}

Many times we feel so self-sufficient and assume we can accomplish everything on our own, even without input from God. We try to achieve major goals, such as going to school to further our education, purchasing a home, planning the perfect wedding and building the ideal family. These endeavors are pursued with the expectation of our heart's desires being fulfilled and all dreams coming to fruition. This is faith in action! We have it. Therefore, although we cannot, physically, see or touch what we want, we believe that if we work relentlessly toward our goals, we will achieve our hearts' desires. We were all given a measure of faith, whether we choose to exercise it physically, spiritually, or neither.

Now faith is the substance of things hoped for, the evidence of things not seen. Hebrews 11:1^{KJV}

We are confident that the efforts we exude or the work we accomplish, using our own strength, will be successful. However, when considering the plans over which we have no control that require dependence on God, we whimper and doubt His abilities. We ask questions such as *Lord, how am I going to pay the bills and send the kids to school? Where will I find another job? Is my 401k safe? What am I going to do without health insurance? What will I do if they take away my pension or social security? God, do you think my marriage can be fixed?* From here, our thoughts spiral out of perspective and negatively affect us in ways-such as loss of sleep, malnutrition, and other varying health issues. It is important to understand that all of these troubles could be prevented with the anchor of our faith being in the will and guidance of the Lord. Our lack of faith implies that God cannot supply our needs, take care of us, or fix our problems.

Beloved, faith is one of the primary tools needed for you to build a relationship with God and to accomplish your goals. I believe faith is the vehicle that will transform your dreams into reality and make your unseen promises tangible. In French, "feid" means "faith, belief, trust, confidence, pledge." Therefore, with confidence, trust God to handle everything you are worried about; and pledge that you will not doubt His abilities. By faith, believe that Jesus Christ is Lord. Believe that He will fulfill all His promises to you. Consider this, He created and protected you from conception until now; so, He is not a man who will deceive or disappoint you. You can trust Him with your life. Your faith in God is activated when you remain steadfast in Him, when you are willing to let everything else go, and when you let Him be in control of your life. As your faith increases, you will have more power and authority over your mind and beliefs. Let today be the day you command the restoration of your faith in God. You now have the faith to believe that Jesus will never leave you nor forsake you. Moreover, your faith is what will activate a mighty move of God on your behalf-rather than murmuring, complaining, or worrying. Faith in God can move mighty mountains and calm raging seas.

Remember, faith is the vehicle that will transform your dreams into reality and make your unseen promises tangible.

Prayer

Dear Heavenly Father,

My soul magnifies You. I reverence Your name. I will praise You, Lord, with every breath I take. I will sing praises unto You, forever. Lord, You are my source of strength, and I worship You. Adonai, I adore Your amazing grace. Oh, faithful God, You are the lifter of my head and my glory. Master, I enjoy the joy that I found in Your presence.

El Selichot, the God who forgives, please forgive me for allowing the voices of the media, political officials, and others to have more influence in my life than You. O, mighty God, I acknowledge that worrying is a sin. In the mighty name of Jesus, please forgive me for allowing worry, panic, and doubt to grip my heart. In the mighty name of Jesus, I ask that You restore and strengthen my faith in You. Jehovah Ez Lami, Lord my strength, help me to depend on You and no one else.

In the mighty name of Jesus, I use the weapon of faith to pull down and destroy the stronghold of fear, doubt, and unbelief. In the mighty name of Jesus, I bind up every evil counsel, demonic sabotage, frustration, and confusion that has interfered with my faith. Elohim, the living God, with great expectation, I look forward to the restoration of my faith so I can please You in all my ways, in Jesus' name. Abba Father, restore unto me the kind of faith that gets Your attention, touches Your heart, and moves Your hands on my behalf, in Jesus' name.

Jehovah, Sel'i, Lord my rock, in the mighty name of Jesus, I stand behind the shield of faith which protects me and quenches the fiery darts of the enemy. O, mighty God, by faith, I dwell in Your secret place–by faith I am hidden under the shadow of Your almighty wings–by faith I go through the valley of the shadow of death and I feared no evil. Everlasting Father, with great faith I believe that You will never leave me nor forsake me, in Jesus' name. Abba Father, with unshakeable faith, I believe You provide for me green pastures and prepare tables filled with excess food in the presence of my enemies.

In the mighty name of Jesus, with unwavering faith, I called that which is impossible to manifest in the realm of possibility. By faith, I believe that You have sent Your angels to encamp around me because I fear You. In the mighty name of Jesus, by faith, I receive Your power to trample the lion, dragon, and adder. By faith, I receive Your anointing to destroy yokes. In the name of Jesus, with unmoveable faith, I declare that the sick and afflicted are healed, the captive is set free, the bands of wickedness are broken, and demonic assignments are canceled in Jesus mighty name. Jehovah Naheh, the God who smites, with bold unwavering faith, in the name of Jesus I curse and cancel every curse, spell, ritual, incantation, caging, and render them powerless, in Jesus' name.

In the mighty name of Jesus, I reject the spirits of fear, doubt, unbelief, worry, and anxiety, and I replace them with faith. Blessed be the Lord, forevermore! In Jesus' mighty name. Amen.

And the Lord said, Simon, Simon, behold, Satan hath desired to have you, that he may sift you as wheat: But I have prayed for thee, that thy faith fail not: and when thou art converted, strengthen thy brethren. Luke 22:31-32^{KJV}

Notes

Week 2

•••

Restore My Appreciation

Therefore I will give thanks unto thee, O Lord, among the heathen, and I will sing praises unto thy name. 2 Samuel 22:50^{KJV}

Many people enjoy the blessings of life: family, friends, food, home, health, wealth, and a land of freedom. However, they never stop to express to God their admiration, acknowledgment, and appreciation of the exceptional work of His hands. My greatest appreciation is the ability to embrace nature. I enjoy being near bodies of water-admiring the characteristics of the ocean, waterfalls, lakes, or even slow streams trickling down never-ending pathways. Often, I stare at the vast blue sky, uniquely punctuated with carefully sculpted clouds; and I stand in the utmost awe at the creativity of God's hands. Other times, I am captivated by the sounds of tweeting birds perched on the limbs of lush green trees with branches that sway gently in the wind. I truly appreciate being awake and able to see, feel, hear, and smell the presence of nature.

What are your cherished moments? Consider this; you beat the odds during y o u r conception. Of the millions of sperm, which were competing to fertilize that one egg, you were chosen to be here. Also, you beat the odds during birth and delivery, because you were not aborted or stillborn. Further, you beat the odds when you survived near-death experiences such as car accidents, sickness, attacks from your enemies, and even suicide attempts. Express your love and gratitude to the Father, and let Him know how much you value Him. While you read this book, someone else is planning a funeral, someone is being hospitalized in an unconscious state, someone is being checked into a psychiatric institution, and someone is pleading for the return of their missing loved one. What is your current state of being? I have known individuals who have suffered great physical loss, but they still express a posture of gratitude and appreciation for simply being alive.

Command the restoration of appreciation to take residence in your life; and thank God for the small gifts surrounding you, regardless of how insignificant they may seem. If you wake up in the morning, it is cause for a thanksgiving party. When you leave your home and return safely, you should engage in both thanksgiving and celebration.

Prayer

Dear Heavenly Father,

I celebrate and appreciate You. How majestic is Your name. Holy Spirit, I value and cherish every moment I spend in Your presence.

Lord, forgive me for being unthankful and ungrateful. O, mighty God, I want to express my appreciation for all things, the pleasurable ones as well as the situations that are displeasing, in Jesus' name.

In the mighty name of Jesus, I use the weapon of appreciation to pull down the stronghold of ungratefulness and unthankfulness, in Jesus' name. With the power in the name of Jesus, I bind up the spirit of ungratefulness. In the name of Jesus, I strip it from its assignment and render it powerless, in Jesus' mighty name. Adonai, my Master and Lord, with great expectations, I look forward to the restoration of my appreciation, in Jesus' name. In the mighty name of Jesus, Father give me a heart that is filled with thanksgiving and appreciation for all that You have given and done for me.

Thank You, Jesus, for life. Almighty God, many times I have taken my five senses for granted and never stop to say how grateful I am that I can see, hear, smell, taste, and feel until something goes wrong. In the mighty name of Jesus, thank You for Your forgiveness. Thank You for salvation. Thank You for dying on the cross for my freedom, in Jesus' name. Thank You for watching over me throughout the years, in Jesus' name. Holy Spirit, thank You for Your unlimited blood covering and protection from the fiery darts of the enemy, in Jesus' name. Lord, thank You for uncommon favor. O Abba Father, thank You for my family, friends, job, wisdom, and understanding, in Jesus' name. Father, I am truly grateful for the restoration of my appreciation. Blessed be the Lord, forevermore! In Jesus' name, Amen.

I will praise thee; for I am fearfully and wonderfully made: marvelous are thy works; and that my soul knoweth right well. Psalm 139:14^{KJV}

WEEK 2 - RESTORE MY APPRECIATION

Notes

Week 3

•••

RESTORE THE SPIRIT OF INTEGRITY

Do not repay anyone evil for evil. Be careful to do what is right in the eyes of everyone. 18If it is possible, as far as it depends on you, live at peace with everyone. Romans 12:17-18^{NIV}

I once listened to a radio program which included two students, Kirk and Lucy. They performed a drama regarding integrity. Kirk was the school president and his character was dishonest. He did not fulfill any of the promises he made during his campaign, yet, he was planning to run for a second term. Lucy, his friend and previous campaign manager, was disappointed. "Kirk, I cannot campaign for you again, and I don't want to be a part of the mess," Lucy said. "Lucy, you are a woman of integrity, and I think you would be the best candidate to run for the presidency," suggested her mentor. "No sir! I cannot do that. Kirk is still my friend. Furthermore, I campaigned for him last year." Her mentor continued, "See Lucy, that is integrity, but knowing what you know, are you going to allow your fellow students to be hurt and deceived again?" Considering this, Lucy decided to run for school president.

When Kirk found out that Lucy would be his opponent, he was furious. He exuded an earnest effort to discredit her during their public debate, and he successfully embarrassed her. She was booed by the crowd. "I believe in integrity, and I will no longer run for school president," Lucy told her mentor. Kirk was elated when he was informed of Lucy's decision. "Kirk, remember Lucy holds your biggest and most crippling secret. She could have done to you what you did to her, but she preferred to bear the humiliation and drop out of the election, rather than exposing your secret. That is integrity, Kirk," the mentor said as he scolded Kirk. Kirk pondered his behavior for a while, and on the day Lucy was going to announce her concession, Kirk hurried to the podium, grabbed the microphone and spoke. "This election is based on integrity, and I am not the person you want to elect for your school president. I am not the person for the job. My opponent is. Given this, I am conceding the election," Kirk announced. Automatically, Lucy became the school president.

May I ask, whose secret did you broadcast because they rubbed you the wrong way? Who do you plan to expose or tear down if they don't do what you ask? Who are you blackmailing because of the secret of theirs which you hold? On whom are you planning to seek revenge? Beloved, integrity demands honesty, loyalty, openness, accountability, and self-awareness. Consider whether your life makes a positive impact on others. Do not play the devil's advocate by rendering evil for evil, but be the bigger person and exhibit integrity. Two wrongs do not make a right.

Allow your moral compass to guide you as you journey through the pathway of life.

Prayer

Dear Heavenly Father,

I celebrate Your name. Jehovah Bara, Lord the Creator, I stand in awe of all Your works and majestic ways. For You are great and do marvelous deeds, and You, alone, are God.

El Elyon, the most high God, create in me a pure heart and renew the right spirit within me. In the mighty name of Jesus, I ask that You Cleanse and purify me with Your blood. Abba, Father, I repent for surrendering my integrity and tarnishing my character for fame and fortune. Lord, in the mighty name of Jesus, please forgive me for misrepresenting Your Word and character. O mighty God, transform me to reflect and represent You in all areas of my life.

Lord, Jesus, You said that whatever I ask in Your name, You will do it and Your Father will be glorified. In the mighty name of Jesus I humbly, ask that You restore my integrity. Jehovah Tsidkenu, God of righteousness, restore unto me moral values and ethics that will speak for me and represent You in a prestigious manner, in Jesus' name. Help me, O God to speak with integrity, walk-in integrity, and conduct business with integrity in Jesus' name.

In the mighty name of Jesus, I use the weapon of integrity to pull down and destroy the stronghold of dishonesty, fraud, and underhandedness. Father, regardless of the consequence, help me to speak the truth, be honest in all my undertakings, and be loyal to You and those who are depending on me as a mentor, in Jesus' name. Lord, with great expectation, I look forward to the restoration of my integrity and character in the mighty name of Jesus. Holy Spirit, help me to develop and practice truth in my inward parts and embrace the importance of integrity and honesty in the mighty name of Jesus. El Gibbor, the mighty God, help me to walk in the spirit so I will not fulfill the lust of the flesh. Father God, I submit my integrity to Your guidance as I make the right choices to exhibit Godly integrity and character in the mighty name of Jesus. Blessed be the Lord, forevermore! In Jesus' mighty name. Amen.

Notes

Week 4

•••

RESTORE MY SELF-WORTH

Before I formed thee in the belly I knew thee; and before thou camest forth out of the womb I sanctified thee, [and] I ordained thee a prophet unto the nations. Jeremiah 1:5^{KJV}

You may feel unworthy. Perhaps, you tell yourself that you are not good enough, you are not pretty enough, and you are not as creative or talented as your friends. You may have considered ending your life because you feel you have no purpose here on earth. Beloved, I personally want to remind you of your pricelessness. Some individuals are late bloomers, and they may discover their purpose, gifts, and talents later in life and become extremely successful. Maybe you are one of those people. Don't give up on becoming the best version of yourself, as you will never discover your worth or value if you quit now.

When life throws you a curveball or you face continuous mishaps, it can be so easy to gravitate towards and succumb to negativity. **Not so fast, Beloved. If you want to know your worth, I will unequivocally tell you, "you are worth dying for."** Someone selflessly gave up His life so you can have and enjoy yours. Someone sacrificed His freedom for yours. Someone suffered brutalization and humiliation for you. Someone made sure you had an unlimited life and health insurance plan, even before you were born. This type of insurance has no expiration date. There is no penalty for late registration, it is not based on your financial status; and, most importantly, it cannot lapse in coverage. That someone is JESUS! Therefore, you should rethink and appeal your thoughts of self-harm and worthlessness. Stand in the mirror and ask yourself these questions; "Who am I?" and "What is my value?" *Ye have not chosen me, but I have chosen you, and ordained you, that ye should go and bring forth fruit, and that your fruit should remain: that whatsoever ye shall ask of the Father in my name, he may give it you. John 15:16*^{KJV}

If you believe you cannot, you won't; but if you believe you can, you will. It is all based on your belief.

Prayer

Dear Heavenly Father,

I worship and adore You. Your greatness is beyond description, and You deserve all the praise, honor, and glory.

El Selichot, the God who forgives, in the mighty name of Jesus, please forgive me of my sin that I have committed. Wash me thoroughly from my iniquities, transgression, and trespasses. In Jesus' name.

Jehovah Bara, my Creator, help me to believe that I am more valuable than the sparrows; I am more cared for than the lilies; I am the apple of Your eye; I am chosen, and I am redeemed. Abba Father, You have numbered every hair on my head. Nothing about me is hidden from You. Therefore, in the mighty name of Jesus, I humbly ask that You restore my self-worth. Father God, help me to see myself the way You see and call me to be, in Jesus' name.

In the mighty name of Jesus, I use the weapon of worthiness to pull down and destroy the strongholds of low self-esteem, self-sabotage, self-hate, and condemnation. Elohim, the living God, according to Romans 8:1, *There is therefore now no condemnation to them which are in Christ Jesus, who walk not after the flesh, but after the Spirit.* O, mighty God, I refuse to condemn myself anymore. With the power in the name of Jesus, I decree and declare that I am hidden in Christ, I am walking after the spirit of the true and living God, and not after the corrupted flesh. Abba Father, with great expectation, I look forward to the restoration of my self-worth. In the mighty name of Jesus.

In the matchless name of Jesus Christ of Nazareth, I rebuke every foul, sabotaging spirit, assigned to distort my self-worth, in Jesus' name. With the power vested in me, I boldly declare that I am worthy; I am valuable; I am fearfully and wonderfully made; and I am the apple of Gods' eye, in Jesus' name. Jesus, Christ of Nazareth, because of my worth, You gave Your life as a ransom for me. O mighty God, Because of my value, You went to hell and took the keys for hell, death, and the grave. Because I am worth it, You walked eighty and two miles with the cross to pay the ransom for my sin. O God, I should have been crucified. I should have suffered and died; but because You saw my worth, You took my place on the old rugged cross at Calvary. Abba Father, because I am worth it, You redeemed my soul and chose for me life everlasting.

In the mighty name of Jesus, I express a heart full of thanks to You, Lord, for opening my eyes to my worth. Thank You for esteeming and affirming me. Thank You for crowning me with Your glory and honor. Almighty God, I appreciate You and love You. Blessed be the Lord, forevermore! In Jesus' name, Amen.

For I know the thoughts that I think toward you, saith the Lord, thoughts of peace, and not of evil, to give you an expected end. Jeremiah 29:11[KJV]

Notes

Week 5

•••

RESTORE MY IDENTITY

*But as many as received him, to them gave he power to become the **sons of God**, even to them that believe on his name. John 1:12^{KJV}*

Many individuals suffer lack in most areas of their lives, living beneath their full potential and feeling inferior. They are excluded from opportunities by individuals of power. Thus, they don't understand their fate, who they really are, or who they were created to be.

Who am I? Have you ever stared in the mirror and asked yourself that question? If someone should ask you the same question, you would generally state your name, where you are from, where you live, your occupation, and maybe your hobbies. Further, you can be identified by your accent, gender, or even habits.

Many individuals believe their careers, accolades, and success define who they are. However, with this mindset, they eventually lose their purpose, potential, and their authenticity. Unfortunately, when their career is over or they are demoted, they are left in disarray, feeling ashamed. Also, given the inability to continue feeding their façade or ego, they become lonely and feel isolated. As a result, they struggle to find their true selves. On the other hand, many people have had their identities stolen by someone trying to impersonate them. Some may have disguised their true identities, trying to be who others want them to be, while others face identity crises, themselves. Additionally, many people have relinquished their identities because they believe what others say about them. Does your character, attitude, behavior, and appearance reflect the personality of God?

Week 5 - Restore My Identity

Identity in Christ Jesus:

Beloved, if your earthly identity was stolen by oppressors, don't worry. It is about to be restored to you, and your thieves will be made to feel inferior and afraid. They would be afraid for you to understand who you truly are, as well as, the power you possess. Jesus died to change your identity from a sinner to a saint and clothe you in His righteousness. You are now a child of God, under His Son-ship. It's okay to take off the camouflage, as you no longer have to disguise who you are or try to fit in where you don't belong. You do not have to believe what the enemy says about you, because you should only believe what your Creator speaks over your life. As a Jesus, blood-washed believer in Christ, you are an heir to God and a joint heir with His Son, Jesus Christ. You are a new creation. You are His temple. You belong to a royal priesthood; and most importantly, you are chosen. Your physical identity was manipulated, but as you lose yourself in Christ, the feelings of inferiority and intimidation will disappear. You will no longer suffer from mistaken identity.

> The closer you draw to God, the more you will discover your true identity and who you are destined to become.

Dear Heavenly Father,

How majestic is Your name. I adore You. You are worthy to be praised. All honor belongs to You, my Father and my God.

In the mighty name of Jesus, I repent of all my sins. Lord, I surrender my heart, mind, body, and soul to You today. Cleanse me from all unrighteousness O God. Purify me with Your blood and set my spirit free from the bondage of sin, in Jesus' name.

Adonai, my Lord and Master, my identity was stolen and sabotaged by the enemy. Father God, in the mighty name of Jesus Christ, I humbly ask that You restore my identity. Abba Father, Your thoughts towards me are always great. O, Mighty God, I know You expect me to be above and not beneath, and to be successful in all my endeavors but I have rejected and ignored who You said I am. Father God, help me not to be men pleaser but to please You at all times.

In the mighty name of Jesus Christ, Satan, I rebuke you and every foul spirit that has come to camouflage and erase my identity. In the mighty name of Jesus, may the fire of God consume every imposter and confederate that have conspired to steal and destroy my identity. In the name of Jesus, may the consuming fire of God destroy every veil and wall that has been positioned to hide my identity. Today, I declare, whenever anyone looks at me, they will see the reflection of Christ. In the mighty name of Jesus, I will be identified as a new creation. I am made new by the blood of the Lamb. In the name of Jesus, open the eyes of the identity stealers so they can see that I serve a God who is still alive and well-a God who chose me to be royalty even before I was formed in my mother's womb.

In the mighty name of Jesus Christ, I rip down and destroy every scroll and banner that has written assignment against my identity. I rise and reclaim my identity. In the mighty name of Jesus, I firmly stand on the Word of God, knowing that I am chosen, I am a peculiar person, and I am a royal priesthood. In the mighty name of Jesus, Satan, may I remind you that before I was formed in my mother's womb, God knew me. He sanctified me and appointed me to be a prophet to the nation. With the power in the Holy Ghost, I strip you of your power to manipulate my mind into believing otherwise. In Jesus' name, Satan, you have lost your privilege to be esteemed; you relinquish your rights to speak to me or in my life. In the mighty name of Jesus, I decree and declare that I am now a friend of God and He calls me a friend. God has identified me as His heir, and joint-heir with His Son, Jesus Christ, and not you. Blessed be the Lord, forevermore! In Jesus' name, Amen.

No, in all these things we are more than conquerors through him who loved us. Romans 8:37^{NIV}

WEEK 5 - RESTORE MY IDENTITY

Notes

Week 6

•••

Restore My Character

Not only so, but we also glory in our sufferings because we know that suffering produces perseverance; 4perseverance, character; and character, hope. 5And hope does not put us to shame, because God's love has been poured out into our hearts through the Holy Spirit, who has been given to us. Romans 5:3-5^{NIV}

Often, individuals self-sabotage by lying, stealing, or being deceptive. Thus, they tarnish their reputations. A vindictive person may also, maliciously, ruin others' character, using slander or accusations. Some individuals ruin their reputations by neglecting their responsibilities to others, by fighting, and by making poor life choices.

Beloved, if your character is blemished, regardless of the reason, it will require the divine intervention of the Holy Spirit for restoration. You must, first, acknowledge and confess to God the wrongs you committed and repent to Him. Repentance before both God and man are the most effective ways to repair your character. You must forgive those who hurt you, but most importantly, you need to forgive yourself. *If we confess our sins, he is faithful and just and will forgive us our sins and purify us from all unrighteousness.* 1 John 1:9^{NIV}

You may have considered that no one will love or trust you again because of your actions. You may think it's useless to try and make amends, but you must surrender your mind to Christ and let Him handle the outcome. Have you ever heard the saying, "It's never too late for a shower of rain"? Jesus specializes in tackling situations that seem impossible. Your reputation will never be so broken that He can't fix it. He will gather the fragmented pieces, put them back together, and create a brand new you. God's love for you is overwhelming and covers a multitude of sins and mistakes. Stop punishing yourself, and let God do His work. *Therefore if any man be in Christ, he is a new creature: old things are passed away; behold, all things are become new. 2 Corinthians 5:17*^{KJV}

Jesus is a character builder; allow Him to rebuild yours.

Prayer

Dear Heavenly Father,

What a mighty God we serve. Lord, You are the King of Kings and the Lord of Lords, and I worship You. Holy Spirit, You are worthy of being magnified and glorified.

O, mighty God, I acknowledge my sin before You. Your Word says he who walks in integrity and with moral character walks securely. Father, in the mighty name of Jesus, I confess that I have tarnished my character because of the bad choices I have made, the wrong people with whom I am associated, and the crooked path I have taken. In the mighty name of Jesus, I seek Your forgiveness for displeasing You with my behavior. Forgive me, O God as I surrender my character to You for a spiritual and physical makeover, in Jesus' name.

Jehovah M'kaddesh, the sanctifier, in the mighty name of Jesus, I humbly ask that You restore within me a Godly character - a character that will represent You anywhere and anytime. O mighty God, restore unto me the kind of character that will cause others to admire and emulate my Godly actions. Abba Father, restore within me the character that will make You proud to call me a friend and servant, in Jesus name.

With the power in the Holy Ghost, I rebuke every spirit of shame and disgrace and I use the weapon of truth to pull down and destroy every spirit that has come to assassinate my character, in Jesus' name.

In the mighty name of Jesus, as of today, I choose to think on things that are true, honest, just, pure, lovely, and of great virtue. Thank You, Holy Spirit, for helping me display Christ-like character that will reflect You in everything that I do and say. Blessed be the Lord forevermore, in Jesus' name, Amen.

A good name is more desirable than great riches; to be esteemed is better than silver or gold. Proverbs 22:1[NIV]

Notes

Week 7

•••

RESTORE MY CONSCIENCE

David was conscience-stricken after he had counted the fighting men, and he said to the Lord, "I have sinned greatly in what I have done. Now, Lord, I beg you, take away the guild of your servant. I have done a very foolish thing. 2 Samuel 24:10[NIV]

The conscience is defined as an inner feeling or voice acting as a guide to the positive behavior of an individual. I compare the conscience to antivirus software, which searches for viruses on the computer, alerts you if any are found, and annihilates them. Likewise, when we engage in immoral or unpleasant acts, our inner voice will whisper. It alerts us that we are on the wrong path, and it makes us feel uneasy until we yield to the proper behavior. The conscience can also be compared to a sensor which sends us a signal when we are being unfair or dishonest to someone else. If we don't hear the trigger of the alarm, or if we don't feel the conviction of our conscience, we are in deep trouble. There may have been times when the spirit of conviction influenced our conscience, but we chose to ignore it, given our desensitization to our own wrongdoings. *And herein do I exercise myself, to have always a conscience void of offence toward God, and toward men.* Acts 24:16[KJV]

Beloved, a fully functioning conscience exposes your position in compliance with the Word of God. You are not living your best life if your conscience is dead. Nonetheless, Jesus Christ, the lover of your soul, still brings dead things back to life. If you reach out to Him and allow Him to take full control of your life, you will become more responsive to the uneasiness you feel when your words or actions are misaligned with His Word. Do not suppress your conscience; it is the voice of your spirit. Do not compromise your integrity to please anyone and suffocate your conscience. You may not be popular or liked when you obey the prompting of your conscience. Do what is right. Hebrews 10:22 KJV. May your conscience be restored to its rightful duty today.

Make sure your conscience is clear with both God and man.

Prayer

Dear Heavenly Father,

I worship You with all my heart. Father, I revere You and bow in humility before You. How majestic is your name in all the earth.

EL Gibbor, Mighty God, I repent from all my sins. Father God, I admit to rejecting the conviction of the Holy Spirit. Forgive me, O God for ignoring His prompting. In Jesus mighty name.

Jehovah Go'el, my redeemer, I know You are the resurrection and the life. I know You specialize in bringing dead things back to life. Therefore, in the mighty name of Jesus, I bring my dead conscience to You, resuscitate my conscience, O God. Through the power in the blood of Jesus Christ, I command my resurrected conscience to alarm as a clock would, when I am participating in immoral acts. Holy Spirit, be my conviction and restore an excellent conscience within me, in Jesus' name. Abba Father, help me not to put away my conscience or turn a blind eye to what is wrong or evil. May my conscience be my guide in Jesus' name.

Through the power in the name of Jesus, I denounce, renounce, and reject any covenant that I made with Satan, known or unknown. In the mighty name of Jesus, I use the weapon of mercy to pull down and destroy every stronghold, inconsideration, and anything else that paralyzed my conscience. Thank You, Abba, for restoring my conscience. Blessed be the Lord, forevermore! In Jesus' name, Amen.

Holding faith, and a good conscience; which some having put away concerning faith have made shipwreck: 1 Timothy 1:19^{KJV}

Notes

Week 8

•••
Restore My Boldness

And now, Lord, behold their threatenings: and grant unto thy servants, that with all boldness they may speak thy word, 30By stretching forth thine hand to heal; and that signs and wonders may be done by the name of thy holy child Jesus. 31And when they had prayed, the place was shaken where they were assembled together; and they were all filled with the Holy Ghost, and they spake the word of God with boldness. Acts 4:29-31^{KJV}

Natural Boldness

Boldness can be used to describe multiple things, including someone's attitude. Some individuals are naturally calm and don't like to engage in confrontation or do anything to hurt another person's feelings. By nature, some are fearful and prefer to play it safe, while some people are obnoxious and defiant. Natural boldness derives from your willingness to do or become whatever you desire. Boldness will encourage you to take risks, many of which can be beneficial in the long-term. Individuals who respectfully exhibit boldness, are not afraid to speak their mind, without using condescending language or tones. They readily admit their failures and weaknesses and don't mind delegating what they cannot manage, themselves. Being bold is also an indicator of confidence; you know what you want, and you recognize failure as an advantage to success. Natural boldness depends on oneself.

Spiritual Boldness

On the other hand, spiritual boldness has nothing to do with one's own efforts but that of the Holy Ghost. There is nothing you can physically do to learn or earn spiritual boldness. Without the unction of the Holy Spirit, you will remain timid. One of my biological sisters is calm-natured, soft-spoken, extremely slow, and fearful. She takes extra precautions not to deliberately hurt anyone. However, when the anointing of God comes upon her, her boldness exudes. With a loud voice, she can be heard commanding demons to abandon their assignments. Once she is prompted by the Holy Spirit to deliver a message from the Lord, it doesn't matter if you are the prime minister, the president, or the queen, she will not hold back. When she does the Lord's work, her fears disappear. However, after the anointing is lifted, fear envelopes her again, much like Elijah, running from one woman (Jezebel) who wanted to kill him after he slew over six hundred of Baal's prophets. The Holy Spirit has to transform you to do what you wouldn't do in the natural. One can be naturally bold but a spiritual coward, while another can be spiritually bold but struggle with fear.

Beloved, God is the ultimate source of spiritual boldness. The lion is called the king of the jungle not because of its size but its boldness. In the world today, you cannot stand by helplessly, and allow the enemy to follow his own agenda on your behalf. You can't afford to be fearful or intimidated. Instead, boldly defend yourself against the wickedness and injustice we will experience in this world.

To equip and empower yourself with spiritual boldness, you should emulate Paul and the disciples, who continuously sought God through prayer. The disciples were not always bold, and one of their prayers for boldness was prayed after the threats they received for preaching in Jesus' name (Acts 4:29-31). Peter and John were once paralyzed with fear, but when they were filled with the Holy Spirit, they were unstoppable. They preached the gospel of Jesus Christ everywhere they went, without compromise. The chief priests and elders marveled at the boldness of Peter and John because they knew Peter and John were unlearned. However, they couldn't deny their power (Acts 4:13).

Read Romans chapter 8 and the book of Acts, and there you will experience how the Holy Spirit empowered the saints with boldness. Beloved, your Holy boldness will give you the courage to reject any ungodly offer from the enemy and stand up for Jesus in the midst of persecution. I pray your spiritual boldness will be restored instantly.

Spiritual boldness depends on how far you are willing to press into the throne room of God.

Below are a few scriptures about boldness which, I hope, will assist you with your prayer for boldness:

In him and through faith in him we may approach God with freedom and confidence. Ephesians 3:12^{NIV}

I eagerly expect and hope that I will in no way be ashamed, but will have sufficient courage so that now as always Christ will be exalted in my body, whether by life or by death. Philippians 1:20^{NIV}

And for me, that utterance may be given unto me, that I may open my mouth boldly, to make known the mystery of the gospel. Ephesians 6:19^{KJV} So that we may boldly say, The Lord [is] my helper, and I will not fear what man shall do unto me. Hebrews 13:6^{KJV}

Now when they saw the boldness of Peter and John, and perceived that they were unlearned and ignorant men, they marvelled; and they took knowledge of them, that they had been with Jesus. Acts 4:13^{KJV}

And when they had prayed, the place was shaken where they were assembled together; and they were all filled with the Holy Ghost, and they spake the word of God with boldness. Acts 4:31^{KJV}

And now, Lord, behold their threatenings: and grant unto thy servants, that with all boldness they may speak thy word. Acts 4:29^{KJV}

The wicked flee when no man pursueth: but the righteous are bold as a lion. Proverbs 28:1^{KJV}

He proclaimed the kingdom of God and taught about the Lord Jesus Christ – with all boldness and without hindrance. Acts 28:31^{NIV}

Prayer

Dear Heavenly Father,

I worship You. You are Alpha and Omega, and I adore You. You are worthy to be praised. Lord, I give You all the glory, honor, and praise. Lord, You are my tower of strength; You are my rock; You are my shield and buckler, and I adore You.

El Elyon, the most high God, in the mighty name of Jesus, I approach Your throne of mercy, seeking forgiveness for every sin that I committed. Cleanse me, O God from all unrighteousness and every sin that easily beset me. Wash and purify me with Your blood, I ask in Jesus' name.

El Elyon, I know that You did not give me the spirit of fear, but I allowed fear to paralyze my boldness to the point where I am afraid to move towards my calling and purpose. Lord, the lack of boldness makes me fearful of speaking in front of an audience or to an individual, by myself. O mighty God, lacking boldness has prevented me from participating in life-changing events. It has prevented me from receiving what is rightfully mine. Father God, I have been taken advantage of because I lack the boldness to stand up for myself. I have been intimidated and look down upon by others. Father God, the lack of boldness caused many to speak to me condescendingly. In the mighty name of Jesus, I crave Your help to express boldness.

In the mighty name of Jesus, I declare that I am as bold as a lion; and I walk with the power and anointing of God to destroy yokes and the spirit of belittlement. In the name of Jesus, I declare that I am more than a conqueror and will not allow myself to be intimidated by anyone again. In the mighty name of Jesus, I use the weapon of boldness and courage to pull down the stronghold of intimidation and fear. I declare that I am brave and fearless. Jehovah Sel'i, Lord, my rock, with great expectation, I look forward to the restoration of my boldness to stand against anyone who tries to make me feel inferior or insignificant. In Jesus' name.

Jehovah Naheh, the Lord who smites, In the name of Jesus, I take authority over the spirit of cowardness, intimidation, and fear. In the mighty name of Jesus, I smite them with the blood and fire of God. In the name of Jesus, I will no longer be a coward or keep silent, but walk and speak with holy boldness through the power of the Holy Ghost. Thank You, Jesus, for restoring my boldness. Thank You for setting me free from the bondage of fear. Blessed be the Lord forevermore! In Jesus' name, Amen.

And the beast was taken, and with him the false prophet that wrought miracles before him, with which he deceived them that had received the mark of the beast, and them that worshipped his image. These both were cast alive into a lake of fire burning with brimstone. Revelation 19:20[KJV]

Week 8 - Restore My Boldness

Notes

Week 9

•••

RESTORE MY DISCIPLINE

No discipline seems pleasant at the time, but painful. Later on, however, it produces a harvest of righteousness and peace for those who have been trained by it. Hebrews 12:11^{NIV}

In an interview, Usain Bolt, the world's fastest man in track and field, shared the rigor of his training routines. He stated, "One may look at you running and say it's easy; it looks effortless, but before it gets to that point, it's hard. It's hard work. It's a day-in, day-out sacrifice." "There were times when I ran, I felt like stopping; I just wanted to give up and say 'to Hell with this, I just want to go home.'" "In the mornings when I woke up knowing that I had intense training, I said 'Oh God, I don't want to go', but I have to make that sacrifice if I want to achieve my dream." During one of his practice sessions, a reporter said, "we are not used to seeing you suffering." Bolt responded, "That's why you guys are here to show the true story." "This here is your reality? Do you mean that the competition is not reality?" The reporter asked. "Listen, the competition is the easiest part. Behind the scene is where all the hard work is done, to get to that one race you need to run for the win," Bolt answered. "Although Bolt is not a morning person, he is awakened at six o'clock almost every morning for training. Some days, he will train two to three times for the day", shared his manager. Bolt continued explaining, "Whenever I don't feel like training, I talk to myself. I am reminded of the promises I made to myself, to become the world's best at what I do." "My goal for winning is my motivation," he concluded.

Bolt's dad made a conscious choice not to watch him during his training any longer, after he had a gut-wrenching experience of his son vomiting after an intense practice. "Son, I didn't know you have to work so hard." Bolt's dad said to him. "I really felt it that day. It's too hard to watch him during the training sessions. He works very hard, and it's a lot of stress on his body; I prefer to watch him at the games, instead," said Bolt's father.

A life without discipline would be tumultuous. The word "discipline" is frequently used, but not many understand the concept or how essential it is in our daily lives. First, discipline requires obedience. Discipline is one of the most crucial attributes needed for success, both physically and spiritually. Can you imagine how disastrous and chaotic this world would be without discipline?

Beloved, even though Bolt would have loved to sleep-in, he denied his flesh the extra sleep so he could achieve his goals and win his gold medals. Given the self-denial and the discipline he demonstrated, he was not controlled by laziness nor lethargy. As a result, the way was paved for his accomplishments. Likewise, to become an extraordinary vessel in the kingdom of God, it takes discipline and self-denial. When you exercise discipline along your Christian journey, you will experience spiritual growth, stability, and structure in your life. Building a unique relationship with Jesus Christ requires discipline. Deny yourself the extra sleep and get into the presence of God at six o'clock each morning for one hour. I can assure you it won't be easy, but you will cultivate discipline, which will help you in every area of your life. Discipline will help you say no to food, stay off the telephone, and keep the television off while fasting.

Most successful individuals earn their titles and accolades because of their discipline and determination. Whenever you witness a man or woman of God cast out demons, prophesy accurately, open blind eyes, profoundly dissect the Word of God, or heal the sick, check their relationship with God. They walk in obedience, and without a doubt, they deny themselves the pleasures and comforts of this world to spend time with God. Exhibiting discipline speaks volumes to your character. It gives you the ability to be the captain of your own ship and a sense of independence, which allows you to be in control of your life, knowing that God completely has your back. In the name of Jesus, I command your discipline to be restored right now.

> Permit discipline to train your mind and character, as you practice obedience.

Prayer

Dear Heavenly Father,

My soul magnifies You. I reverence Your name. I will praise You, Lord, with every breath I take. I will sing praises unto You, forever. Lord, You are my source of strength, and I worship You.

Jehovah Tsidkenu, my righteousness, I repent of all my sins, known and unknown. Wash me thoroughly and cleanse me with Your blood in Jesus' name. O mighty God, forgive me for being so in love with my flesh that I ignored Your command to exhibit and promote discipline in my life.

Father, in the mighty name of Jesus, I confess that my self-discipline has completely deteriorated physically, and spiritually. Lord, due to the lack of discipline I have forfeited my dreams and visions. O, mighty God, the lack of discipline caused me to run from challenging tasks, fail to succeed, lose focus, and become spiritually and financially retarded. O Father God, the lack of discipline caused me to become the victim instead of the victor. It makes me settle for mediocrity and ruin great opportunities. Father God, the lack of discipline has blocked my prosperity and caused me to be unproductive and comfortable in my situations. Adonai, my Lord and Master, with Your rod of correction, remove the folly of indiscipline away from my heart.

In the mighty name of Jesus, I seek the restoration of self-discipline. Through the power in the blood of Jesus Christ, I use the weapon of discipline to pull down and destroy the stronghold of indiscipline, so that I may walk under the leadership of Christ without compromising His words. In the mighty name of Jesus, I decree and declare that stability and structure are restored in my life through the restoration of self-discipline.

Father God, give me the discipline to read Your Word, fast, and pray without yielding to distractions. In the name of Jesus, I command my flesh to be subjected to the Holy Spirit as I bow in reverence to You. In the name of Jesus, Father God, grant me the discipline to resist answering the phone while I am praying. Give me the discipline to resist checking my WhatsApp, email, Instagram, or messages before I speak to You or get out of bed in the mornings. In the mighty name of Jesus, help me to promote discipline and stay focused in Your presence. O mighty God, help me to make sacrifices that are beneficial to my spirit-man. Blessed be the Lord forevermore! In Jesus name. Amen.

Whoever heeds discipline shows the way to life, but whoever ignores correction leads others astray. Proverbs 10:17[NIV]

DAILY RESTORATIONAL

Notes

_____ *Week 10*

•••

Restore My Humility

Therefore, as God's chosen people, holy and dearly loved, clothe yourselves with compassion, kindness, humility, gentleness and patience. Colossians 3:12^{NIV}

Compromising the Word of God to spare the feelings of those who need to hear the truth is not a demonstration of humility. Humility is one of the highest virtues and the most amazing quality you can possess; however, it is challenging to cultivate. Acknowledging your unworthiness and understanding God's ownership over everything you possess and have accomplished is the epitome of humility. Humility will also encourage you to accept God as the sole source of your help and not as an additional resource. A humble person who understands their identity doesn't have to compete with others, fight to be recognized, or seek approval to feel validated, as they will never try to impress anyone. Humility will make you admit that you are not self-made but that you were granted the privilege and opportunity by God to become who you are today. It is understood that humility is the opposite of pride, and wherever pride is, disgrace closely follows. Being humble enough not to think of yourself as superior to someone else is important. Instead, assist them so they can achieve greatness.

Beloved, unless you humbly submit to God, He won't be able to use you to the fullness of your abilities. If it's your desire to prosper over the enemy, you must be pliable in the hand of God. You must understand that, unless He intervenes in your affairs, you will inevitably fail, as you are nothing without Him. Humility requires surrendering your heart, mind, and thoughts to the superior power of God; and He will exalt you beyond your comprehension. There is a song that says "If I'm too high Lord, please bring me down." May that be your request as well. Being humble will allow your gifts to make room for you, and great men will be subdued by the power of God within you, as they bow in humility, anxiously wanting to know what the Lord has to say about them.

Be thankful for everything in life, understanding that it is not your doing but the gift of God.

Prayer

Dear Heavenly Father,

I will bless You, O my soul, and all that is within me. Bless Your holy name. Lord, how excellent is Your name in all the Earth. I give You all the praise and glory. Lord, my soul magnifies You, adores You, reveres You, and glorifies You.

Jehovah Gibbor, You are the mighty God. I confess that the absence of humility has open the door for my heart, mind, and spirit to be lifted up with pride. It has caused me to trespass against many of my sisters and brothers, leaving them emotionally and spiritually wounded. Forgive me, O God. Father God, Your Word says that pride goes before destruction. In the mighty name of Jesus, help me not to be destroyed in my folly. O, mighty God, I seek Your forgiveness for the many souls I have caused to go astray because of my stuck-up attitude and prideful behavior. Father God, the lack of humility made me think that I am too high to humble myself before You and man. Lord, I repent in Jesus' name.

In the mighty name of Jesus, I ask that You restore the spirit of humility within me. In the name of Jesus, I use the weapon of humility to pull down and destroy the stronghold of pride. In the mighty name of Jesus, I surrender my heart, mind, and soul to the Holy Spirit. God, with humility, and a heart filled with gratitude, I say thank You Lord for the restoration of my humility, in Jesus' name. Blessed be the Lord, forevermore! In Jesus' name, Amen.

When pride comes, then comes disgrace, but with humility comes wisdom. Proverbs 11:2^{NIV}

Notes

Week 11

•••

RESTORE MY WILL-POWER

For I do not do the good I want to do, but the evil I do not want to do – this I keep on doing. Romans 7:19^{NIV}

Have you ever tried extremely hard not to give in to something, but before you knew it, you had already submitted? Lacking will-power may also mean that you lack discipline, determination, and self-control. In the absence of will-power, habits become hard to break; struggles are more challenging to overcome; thoughts seem impossible to restrain, and emotions are tricky to control. Losing your will-power is like an out of control car or a ship without its navigation system- drifting aimlessly. Ultimately, there is no drive to try and correct the situation.

Many have lost the will to live. Some have lost the determination to succeed, and others have lost the discipline to abstain from harmful situations. You may have heard individuals cry out in, seemingly, hopeless desperation because they want to quit specific habits but feel helpless. Some individuals want to lose weight or stop smoking, gambling, drinking, lying, stealing, committing adultery, or fornicating, but the more they try to quit, the tighter they feel a stronghold.

Beloved, to reach spiritual altitude, your physical attitude must be submitted. Yield your self-willed attitude to God. The restoration of your will-power recognizes **your willingness** to identify your weaknesses and strongholds which hold you back and conquers them. Your determination will be required to overcome your most challenging obstacles when both your mind and body want to give up. Restoring will-power means taking control of your will, as you **practice and train** your mind and flesh to stray from what is disastrous to your health and well-being. Finally, you must cultivate the discipline to continually refrain from bad habits. I understand your spirit may be willing to make the changes, but your flesh fights back. Do not forget you can do anything you set your mind to. God will give you strength.

Be intentional.

Prayer

Dear Heavenly Father,

I adore You. I magnify Your Holy and sweet name. Lord, You are the lifter of my head. You are my strength when I am weak. You are my strong tower, my shield, and my buckler. Glory to God, Holy Spirit, I welcome You into my space and into my life. God, I celebrate You. Lord, I love You beyond measure. Thank You for being awesome.

Lord, I surrender my heart to You right now. Take out all ill-feelings, unforgiveness, resentment, or bitterness that is hidden within me. Lord, I repent of all my sins; please forgive me, in Jesus' name.

Elyashiv, the God who restores, my enthusiasm to succeed has diminished. The will-power to fight my addictions, to say no to food, and to eat right, has died. O, mighty God, it seems as if I have lost the will-power to live, the will-power for self-care, and the will-power to work. Lord, I have lost the will-power to give birth to my dreams and fulfill my visions. In the matchless name of Jesus, I am crying out for help. Hear my cry from Your sanctuary, O Lord, and restore unto me the will-power to rise above discouragement and be who You ordained me to be. Father God, give me the courage to pursue my dreams again. In Jesus mighty name.

Week 11 - Restore My Will-Power

Jehovah Mephalti, my deliverer, I use the weapon of determination to pull down and destroy the stronghold of depression, oppression, and disappointment, in the name of Jesus. May the blood of Jesus Christ paralyze every foul spirit that is assigned to sabotage my will-power, in Jesus' name. May the consuming fire of Jehovah Naheh, the God who smites, destroy all evil works against my will-power in Jesus' name.

In the mighty name of Jesus, I send arrows of fire into the enemy's camp to destroy every demonic altar erected against my will-power. Father God, You said whatever I bind on Earth, You will bind it in heaven, and whatever I loose on earth, You will loose in heaven. Father God, with that instruction, I bind up principalities, I bind powers, and I bind spiritual wickedness in high and low places that seek to exalt themselves against my will-power. In Jesus' name.

O mighty God, thank You for restoring my will-power so I can move freely to pursue my purpose, in Jesus' mighty name. Thank You, God, for restoring my enthusiasm for life, again. Thank You for the deliverance, in Jesus' name. Blessed be the Lord, forevermore! Amen and Amen.

There hath no temptation taken you but such as is common to man: but God is faithful, who will not suffer you to be tempted above that ye are able; but will with the temptation also make a way to escape, that ye may be able to bear it. 1 Corinthians 10:13^{KJV}

DAILY RESTORATIONAL

Notes

Week 12

•••

RESTORE MY SELF-CONTROL

Like a city whose walls are broken through is a person who lacks self-control. Proverbs 25:28 ^{NIV}

*S*elf-control has been defined as a vital skill that needs to be honed daily to be effective. Also, it is the ability to manage your behavior, feelings, and emotions. When the power of self-control is refined, one can restrain themselves from various temptations, such as sudden outbursts of anger, aggressive behavior, and impulsivity. Further, with self-control, there is no desire to seek revenge against or sabotage anyone, regardless of their actions. The distinguishing qualities of self-control encourage conscientiousness, organization, and efficiency at all tasks.

Perhaps you struggle to control yourself from multiple attacks of the flesh, but you have suppressed the struggles for years. Despite this hardship, if you are ready for your deliverance, today is your day to be delivered. Can you identify your struggles? Maybe you struggle to control your appetite for food or sex, your tongue from lying, your eyes from lusting, your temper from flaring, and your mind from thinking negatively. There may be more, but you no longer have to succumb to these attacks.

Beloved, remember that self-control is a fruit of the spirit. Therefore, with sincerity and humility, invite God into every crevice and corner of your heart, mind, and spirit. Without pride and on bent knees, pour out to Him all that controls you and hinders your spiritual growth. Don't hold back. Once you expose the enemy, he has no more secrets for you. Express to God how losing self-control has interfered with your relationship with Him, as well as with your life daily. I encourage you to seek God for your deliverance from anything that removes you from His perfect will.

Jesus is a baggage handler. He will never charge you for the extra pieces; and He will never tell you you're overweight. Check-in your baggage with Him today.

Prayer

Dear Heavenly Father,

You are amazing and superb, You are awesome. Thank You for being my God. You are my Master and my King. Lord, I wouldn't trade You for anyone else. God, it is such a glorious feeling to be in Your presence.

Father God, forgive me for not managing my feelings, emotions, and behavior in a Godly way. In the mighty name of Jesus, I ask that you forgive me for not exercising self-control. Father God, I confess that lacking self-control has cost me some dear friends, my job, my peace, my joy and has interfered with my salvation. Adonai, I have made some poor decisions because I was unable to control my anger. Father God, the loss of self-control has posed a challenge to resist temptations in so many areas of my life.

In the mighty name of Jesus, I command self-control to be restored unto me right now. In the name of Jesus, I use the weapon of self-control to pull down and destroy the strongholds of anger, aggressiveness, impulsiveness, and any other temptations. In the name of Jesus Christ of Nazareth, I bind these spirits and loose the spirit of organization and conscientiousness in my life.

Week 12 - Restore My Self-Control

EL Shaddai, in the name of Jesus, I ask that You would restore my self-control. Give me the wisdom to be Holy-Spirit led, governed, and controlled in everything I do and say, in Jesus' mighty name. Thank You, Lord, for the restoration of my self-control, in Jesus' name. Blessed be the Lord, forevermore! In Jesus' name, Amen.

Be sober, be vigilant; because your adversary the devil, as a roaring lion, walketh about, seeking whom he may devour: 1 Peter 5:8^{KJV}

DAILY RESTORATIONAL

Notes

_____ *Week 13*

•••

Restore My Health & Memory

Then God said, "I give you every seed-bearing plant on the face of the whole earth and every tree that has fruit with seed in it. They will be yours for food. Genesis 1:29^{NIV}

*H*ave you noticed any changes regarding your health or memory lately? If so, do you know you have the power to call forth a healthy memory and speak life and wholeness into your body? Your body is the temple of the Lord, and if He lives within you, sickness should not have a place to grow or spread in your body, resulting in death. Healing is God's desire for His children who believe, obey, and follow His instructions regarding what we should and shouldn't do, or what we should and shouldn't eat. Beloved, I wish above all things that thou mayest prosper and be in health, even as thy soul prospereth. 3 John 1:2^{KJV}

They shall take up serpents; and if they drink any deadly thing, it shall not hurt them; they shall lay hands on the sick, and they shall recover. Mark 16:18^{KJV}

In this verse, God says you may find yourself in grave danger, but He will be with you, and you are protected. You serve a God who does not change. He is consistent in the fulfillment of His promises. Though the atmosphere may be riddled with viruses, bacteria, pollution, and other ailments, you may go unaffected. Also, though illnesses can be caused by various agents, countless infirmities are caused by demonic affliction, while some are self-induced, caused by disobedience. God has given you a manual (the Bible) to follow; but if you refuse to open it, read it, and apply it, your body can be subject to infirmities caused by spiritual "bullets".

Beloved, though the Lord has equipped the doctors and pharmacists with the knowledge to repair defective body parts, surgery and medications do not have to be your only source of healing. Activate your faith and trust that God can and will do what He promised. Most healing may be delayed because of doubt, unbelief, and lack of faith. The same faith with which you trust your doctor and pharmacist, if transferred even slightly to the Holy Ghost, will reveal amazing feats. Healing can be yours today, if you surrender your belief system to God.

Prayer

Dear Heavenly Father,

I stand in awe when I look at creation and think about Your creativity. You deserve to be praised. How unique and awesome You are. Father God, You are indescribable.

Lord, I admit that I have been disobedient to Your instructions regarding how to eat and take care of my body. God, I confess that I have opened many doors, giving Satan permission to afflict my memory and my health. Forgive me, O God

Father, I ask that You restore my health.

Father God, I know Your desire is for me to prosper and be in good health. In the mighty name of Jesus, I ask that You would restore my health and memory. Jehovah Rophe, my healer, please forgive me for the terrible health decisions I have made, which cause sickness to invade my temple. In the mighty name of Jesus, I speak to every organ, system, blood vessel, bone, and cell in my body, and I command them to come into divine alignment with how You created them to function, in Jesus' name. Father God, You said that You sent your Word to heal all disease. In the mighty name of Jesus, I declare that no disease, virus, bacteria, or any form of infirmity or affliction shall have dominion over my body. Elohim, Your Word declares that healing is Your children's bread. Abba Father, in the mighty name of Jesus, I receive healing in every area of my body through Your Word. Lord Jesus, by Your stripes, I know that I am healed in my mind, body, and spirit, in Jesus' mighty name.

Father, I ask that You would restore and sharpen my memory.

In the mighty name of Jesus Christ, I use the weapon of healing to pull down and destroy all forms of mental, physical, and emotional illness. Father God, You told us to call those things that are not as if they were. Therefore, in the mighty name of Jesus, today, I decree and declare that I am not forgetful. My memory is always sharp, in Jesus' name. I declare that my memory operates in full capacity. In the name of Jesus, Alzheimer's, dementia, insanity, depression nor any form of mind-altering illness will never be my portion, in Jesus' mighty name. Through faith, I receive the restoration and healing of my health and memory, in Jesus' name. Blessed be the Lord, forevermore! Amen.

But unto you that fear my name shall the Sun of righteousness arise with healing in his wings; and ye shall go forth, and grow up as calves of the stall. Malachi 4:2[KJV]

Notes

Week 14

•••

Restore My Strength

So do not fear, for I am with you; do not be dismayed, for I am your God. I will strengthen you and help you; I will uphold you with my righteous right hand. Isaiah 41:10^{NIV}

Today may be one of those days when you don't want to get out of bed or leave the house. Perhaps you were disappointed that daybreak came so quickly. Your limbs feel lifeless, and your energy feels zapped. Motivation and inspiration are scarce, and hopelessness has taken a front-row seat. You feel overwhelmed trying to safely ride the roller coaster of life, while thoughts of quitting bombard your mind.

Negative news, announcing senseless killings, missing children, and invasions of privacy, can contribute to overall energy loss. Loss of strength can also be caused by your children's rebellion, rejection from friends, criticism, neglect, or overall persecution from others.

Beloved, the bible says when the weakest of saints go on their knees to pray, the devil trembles. Do not listen to the whispering demons. Instead, seek to restore the joy of the Lord, since it is written that the joy of the Lord is your strength. Identify the root cause for the deterioration of your strength so you will know how to direct your prayer and bind the assignment of the enemy over your life. Your strength may be weakened, but your mind is still alert, and you are stronger than you believe you are. Rise above your feelings and command your inner strength to emerge from its place of retirement and be restored unto you. Regardless of what may have zapped your strength, do not grieve, for God's strength will be made perfect in your weakness. *He giveth power to the faint; and to them that have no might he increaseth strength. Isaiah 40:29*^{KJV}

I command unlimited strength to be restored to your body right now. God is the source of your strength, your strong tower, the lifter of your head, and your restorer.

> Tap into God's presence now, and be strengthened in Jesus' mighty name.

Prayer

Dear Heavenly Father,

Jehovah 'Uzam, Lord My Strength, You have been my strength in the time of trouble. You are my rock, my shield, and my hiding place. Lord, You are all I need. You are glorious. Abba, Father, how great and holy You are. I exalt Your name on high. Blessed be Your name in all the Earth.

In the mighty name Jesus, I repent of all my sins. I repent for relying and depending on my own strength. Wash me thoroughly from all impurities, iniquities, and every sin that easily besets me, in Jesus' mighty name.

In the mighty name of Jesus Christ of Nazareth, I use the weapon of strength to pull down and destroy the spirit of lethargy, weakness, and fatigue, in Jesus' name. Abba Father, thank You for restoring my physical and spiritual strength, . Thank You, God, for renewing my strength so I can mount up with wings like an eagle, in Jesus' name. O, mighty God, You promised that Your strength will make perfect in my weakness. Thank You for the strength to run this Christian race and not fail, in Jesus' name. Thank You, Jesus, for the strength to walk, without fainting. In the mighty name of Jesus, I reclaim my strength to run through troops and leap over walls that are erected to stop me.

Week 14 - Restore My Strength

El Manzi, God of strength, thank You for the strength to face another day, in Jesus' name. Thank You for the strength to face my opposition. Father God, thank You for being the source of my strength, in Jesus' name. Thank You for being my refuge and strong tower. O mighty God, thank You for the strength to stand against those who rise against me, in Jesus' name. Thank You, Lord, for the strength to overcome heartbreak and trials, in Jesus' name. Father God, as I lay at Your feet, hide me in Your secret place. In the mighty name of Jesus, I release the angels who excel in strength at the Word of God to encamp around me and deliver me, in Jesus' name.

Blessed be the Lord, forevermore! In Jesus' name, Amen.

The Lord is my strength and my defense; he has become my salvation. He is my God, and I will praise him, my father's God, and I will exalt him. Exodus 15:2^{NIV}

DAILY RESTORATIONAL

Notes

_____ *Week 15*

•••
Restore My Years

And I will restore to you the years that the locust hath eaten, the cankerworm, and the caterpiller, and the palmerworm, my great army which I sent among you. ²⁶And ye shall eat in plenty, and be satisfied, and praise the name of the Lord your God, that hath dealt wondrously with you: and my people shall never be ashamed.

Joel 2:25-26^{KJV}

Many years ago, when my son was in culinary school, he was chosen as the sous-chef, which allowed him to enter a cooking challenge, and he won. After that competition, he and a fellow student chef were awarded the opportunity to participate in a television cooking show contest. Unfortunately, my son fell ill, and because he led the charge as head chef, the student chef was unable to participate. They both missed the chance to showcase their cooking skills on television, which was disappointing. As I comforted my son, I reassured him that one day he would get the chance to share his gourmet cooking expertise on TV, even if it required me to host my own television program.

Today, God expresses the same sentiment. Every opportunity you missed will be restored back to you, full circle. Regardless of whether it was stolen, damaged, hijacked, or destroyed, your hopes and dreams will not go overlooked. When the enemy took your ideas and blocked the opportunities presented to you, you gave up on yourself. You became unproductive, you quit fighting to prosper, and you relinquished your power to him. Perhaps you re-considered the benefits of being a Christian and remaining loyal to God. You may have even asked yourself if it is worth it to continue living. You may consider yourself a failure because you haven't accomplished everything you hoped to. Yes, you were deceived, which left you disappointed, but you will now be restored.

You still have the potential to be successful and achieve great things. Dismiss the idea that you are too old, that you will never receive another opportunity, or that you will never have enough money to make your dreams a reality. If God gave you the vision, He will make the provision. Daniel had to pray his promised gift/answer out of the enemy's grip. God is preparing to restore your missed opportunities alongside additional blessings. Today, God will intervene in your situation once you return to Him, fully and sincerely. The blessings He will restore to you will present as if you never lost anything in the first place. God restored a double portion of blessings unto His servant Job, so will He restore you. He will redeem the time you lost.

Accelerate your prayers and release your angels to fight for you.

Prayer

Dear Heavenly Father,

How beautiful You are. You are Emanuel, God with us. You are an ever-present help in my time of trouble. You are my blessed Redeemer. All glory, honor, and praise belong to You. All glory belongs to You, forever. O Sovereign God, I vow to give You the glory. Don't take Your spirit away from me. Fill me up Lord, until I overflow. I give You all of me. I surrender myself to You.

1 John 1:8 says, *If we say that we have no sin, we deceive ourselves, and the truth is not in us.* Father God, I confess, I have sinned against You and the instructions of Your Word; forgive me. Adoni, my Lord, and Master, I repent for all the years I've walked in unforgiveness, bitterness, resentment, hatred, malice, envy, jealousy, selfishness, pride, lust, gossip, and tale-bearing. Cleanse me, O God from all iniquities and impurities. Detox my heart, O God, in Jesus mighty name.

Week 15 - Restore My Years

Abba, Father, I have lost time, I have lost opportunities, I have lost favor, and I have lost optimism for my future. O, mighty God, I stand on Your promises believing that You will restore my years and the years that the locust, the cankerworm, the caterpillar, and the palmerworm had eaten. In the mighty name of Jesus, I use the weapon of prayer to pull down and destroy every stealing, sabotaging spirit that sabotaged my destiny, purpose, and the plan of God for my life.

Jehovah Go'el, God, my Redeemer, thank You for redeeming the time that I have lost, in Jesus' name. Lord, I will place my trust in You, to open doors that no man can close. Father God, I trust Your timing and I trust You with my heart. Blessed be the Lord, forevermore! In Jesus' name, Amen.

And ye shall eat in plenty, and be satisfied, and praise the name of the Lord your God, that hath dealt wondrously with you: and my people shall never be ashamed. Joel 2:26^{KJV}

DAILY RESTORATIONAL

Notes

Week 16

•••

Restore My Marriage

Wives, submit yourselves unto your own husbands, as it is fit in the Lord. Husbands, love your wives, and be not bitter against them.
Colossians 3:18-19^{KJV}

Many times we make the mistake of settling for *Mr. or Mrs. "Right Now"*, rather than diligently waiting on the Lord to send the right person who He ordained for us.

An unwed couple may have lived together for many years but the moment they decided to honor God's Word by getting married, they began experiencing unbearable challenges. Unfortunately, within months of saying *I do*, their marriage ended. Why? When they were committing fornication (sin) they were honoring Satan's command, hence he allowed them to feel comfortable in sin as if everything was okay.

Marriage is an institution created by God for man and must operate under God's divine instruction. Sadly, marriages fall apart for various reasons, including a lack of foundation, morals, communication, and respect. In addition, many marriages end because of third-party interference from in-laws, friends, or extramarital affairs. The list is exhaustive.

Many people become impatient with marriage and pursue a spouse whom God did not choose. Disappointingly, they ultimately determine they made a big mistake. This doesn't mean either person is bad; they just weren't meant for each other. Some spouses stay together for their children, some stay to avoid embarrassment and criticism, while some stay because they figure a divorce alternative is more expensive. Overall, when we disobey God to satisfy the flesh, it will cost us dearly.

Before you command the restoration of your marriage, you must ask yourself a few important questions regarding your spouse:

- Was this person sent by God? Were they my choice or God's choice?
- Are we supposed to be married?
- Did I force this marriage?
- If I take them back, will I still suffer abuse? Will they still be unfaithful or leave again?
- Did I ignore the warning signs not to marry them?
- Why were they in my life? Was it to help me up or bring me down?
- God, are they the one for me? Were we sharing responsibilities, equally?
- Was I respected, loved, satisfied, happy, and comfortable in the marriage?
- Was this a one-sided relationship? In other words, am I forcing someone to love and be with me, out of guilt or obligation?

Many years ago, I listened to Pastor Layton Smith on his "Count Down" Friday night radio program. He stated that, while seated on an airplane, next to him sat a beautiful young lady with whom he wanted to speak, but he was uncertain how to initiate the conversation. However, he said when dinner was served, he noticed she refused the food. "Why are you not eating?" Layton asked. "I am fasting," she responded. That broke the ice. "What denomination are you, and for what reason are you fasting?" asked Layton. "I am a witch; we are fasting to break up marriages," she answered.

Beloved, if there is a rift in your marriage, caused by the interference of a third party, now is the time to command the restoration of your marriage with authority and assertiveness. If you know your spouse is from God and you are meant to be together, use the Word of God to proclaim unity over your marriage. Marriage is a solemn covenant not to be entered into lightly. Don't get married just for sex, to have someone to make you happy, or to satisfy your lustful desires. Getting married for any of the above reasons can cause disaster and divorce. It will be difficult for your expectations to be met. A Christ-centered, Spirit-filled marriage will last a lifetime, despite the opposition. Divorce not only hurt individuals but entire families as well, so be sure to put God first.

> Divorce is not the answer. See each other how you would like God to see you. Learn to compromise.

Prayer

If your marriage is whole, pray for someone else's marriage.

Dear Heavenly Father,

You are worthy of my praise, worthy of being exalted, and worthy of being honored. You deserve the glory and the honor; and I lift my hands in worship to You. I exalt Your glorious and matchless name.

Father God, I repent for the sins I committed against my spouse. Forgive me for harboring resentment, bitterness, unforgiveness, hate, and anger. I repent for not valuing the covenant of marriage. I admit that the foundation of my marriage has not been built on Your Word.

Jehovah Hoshe'ah, You are the God who saves. In the name of Jesus, I ask that You restore and save my marriage. Lord, I place my marriage in Your hands. Father God, restore our love and affection for each other. In the mighty name of Jesus, restore honesty, loyalty, and respect. Father, help us to communicate effectively as two mature adults who fear You and desire to please You. Reignite the fiery passion in our marriage, O God.

In the name of Jesus, I use the weapon of fasting and prayer to rip down and destroy every foul spirit, curse, spell, and ritual done against my marriage. Through the power of the Holy Ghost, I bind up the spirit of separation and divorce, confusion, and hate. In the mighty name of Jesus, I cancel every evil assignment against my marriage. I declare that my marriage is a reflection of Christ. In the mighty name of Jesus, my marriage will be an example to others around us.

Through the power in the blood of Jesus, I command the passion and fire to be reignited in my marriage and all marriages ordained by You. In the mighty name of Jesus, I speak life, love, joy, respect, communication, and friendship into every God-ordained marriage. Father God, Your Word said that who You joined together, let no man break asunder. Blessed be the Lord, forevermore! In Jesus' name, Amen.

The Lord shall cause your enemies who rise up against you to be defeated before your face; they shall come out against you one way and flee before you seven ways. Deuteronomy 28:7

Week 16 - Restore My Marriage

Notes

Week 17

•••

RESTORE MY FAMILY

Bear with each other and forgive one another if any of you has a grievance against someone. Forgive as the Lord forgave you.
Colossians 3:13^{NIV}

A family that prays together stays together. In general, families are prone to have disagreements. This is also true, biblically, given the stories of Cain and Able, Joseph and his brothers, David and his son, Absalom, Moses, and his sister, Miriam, and the list continues.

Though the COVID-19 pandemic has been catastrophic, many families were forced to spend time with each other. What the devil meant for our destruction, God uses to bring people together, especially families. I hope God has been revealed to you during this disaster. It would be regrettable if you didn't use this opportunity to build a bond with your family. If it takes a global pandemic to mend our hearts and change our behavior, God will allow it because He loves us, unconditionally.

God placed us in our families for a reason. Whether we acknowledge it or not, many of us would not be where or who we are without our families. I do understand that some family members can be challenging to tolerate. However, consider the despicable things we have done which displeases God. Think of the many times we hurt His feelings, yet He still wakes us up in the mornings, provides our daily necessities, and shields us from the devil's wrath. Do we deserve His help?

Week 17 - Restore My Family

Beloved, there will come a day when we won't be able to reach each other by phone, Facebook, email, WhatsApp, or by any other form of social media anymore. All communication will be cut off, and we will be forced to separate from friends and families. Therefore, make today the day you let go of unforgiveness, anger, and resentment. Seek forgiveness and restoration for your family. Be sure to address all unresolved issues. It doesn't matter how often you may visit the gravesite of a deceased loved one, because it is impossible to reconcile with them after death. If you refuse to humble yourself and make amends now, sadly, you will be the one living with torment later. Swallow your pride, remove the hardness from your heart, and mend things with your loved ones before it's too late. Jesus will soon return for His second coming. You have come too far not to make it to your promised land. Therefore if thou bring thy gift to the altar, and there rememberest that thy brother hath ought against thee; 24Leave there thy gift before the altar, and go thy way; first be reconciled to thy brother, and then come and offer thy gift. Matthew 5:23-24KJV The rift between you and your family members can be repaired. Take a moment to reflect on the cause of the animosity. Consider: Does the reason make sense? Can you explain what happened? Was it a misunderstanding? Did you confront the individual to find out the truth? Given that the enemy knows the importance of family and how much God embraces family unity, he schemes and uses various tactics to sabotage families.

If you are not holding resentment and unforgiveness, you should be the peacemaker in your family and facilitate emotional repair. Learn how to identify when the devil is at work, and then, rebuke and resist him.

> Don't dwell on how your family treats you. Instead, ask yourself, "How do I treat my family?"

Prayer

Dear Heavenly Father,

I honor You. I appreciate You, and I thank You for Your guidance. Lord, You are holy, righteous, and great. You are a miraculous God. There is no one else like You. You deserve the glory and honor. I worship You with all my heart, and I magnify Your name.

Lord, as I present my heart to You today, I confess that I have been harboring wickedness in my heart towards my family. Forgive me, O God, as I repent from this ungodly behavior. Cleanse my heart that I may get rid of anger, bitterness, and unforgiveness that I feel towards them. Abba Father, in the name of Jesus, help me to let go of the hurt and pain that I have suffered at the hands of my family. Reveal to me everyone who I am holding hostage in my heart so I can seek their forgiveness, Lord. In the mighty name of Jesus, I want to make heaven my home. Therefore, please forgive me and cleanse me from all ill feelings, in the mighty name of Jesus.

Father, in the name of Jesus, I ask that You restore my family. Lord, according to Proverbs 21:1, the heart of the king is in the hand of the Lord, and like the river, you can turn it anywhere you choose. Abba, You created my family, so please turn their hearts back to You. In the name of Jesus, deliver them from the snares of the enemy. Oh Sovereign God, there is nothing too hard for You. Jehovah Shammah, I know You are present in the life and affairs of my family. In the name of Jesus, I ask that You deliver them from generational and bloodline curses and the nets set by the enemy. In the mighty name of Jesus, I know the enemy is trying very hard to separate our family and ruin our relationship with You, as well as, with each other. Jehovah 'Uzam, You are our strength in times of trouble, and unity is strength. O Father God, unite and strengthen the bond between us again, so we can defeat the enemy.

In the mighty name of Jesus, I use the weapon of peace to pull down and destroy the rift in my family's life. In the name of Jesus, I bind

Week 17 - Restore My Family

up every stronghold that is preventing my family from enjoying and embracing each other. I bind every contrary, confusing, malicious, and frustrating spirit assigned to cause chaos and confusion in my family. I bind every generational and bloodline curse from both maternal and paternal sides. I call my family redeemed and reconciled back to the Father, in Jesus' mighty name.

If the Rift doesn't Involve you, Pray this Prayer

Dear Eloah,

My God, I come boldly before You on behalf of my family. Lord, the enemy has crept in and placed a gigantic rift between the family, causing them to be at war with each other. Father, I recognize the enemy is at work. Father God, I pray that You will open the eyes of my family so they can see who is behind this wickedness. Jehovah Izoa, thank You for the restoration of my family. Thank You that my family is healed, made whole, delivered, and washed in the blood of Jesus Christ. The love of God is flowing through the hearts of my family towards each other. Thank You, Jesus, for restoring my family.

Thank You for being with my family and me. Thank You for breaking every fetter and setting us free, in Jesus' mighty name. Blessed be the Lord, forevermore! In Jesus' name, Amen.

I appeal to you, brothers and sisters, in the name of our Lord Jesus Christ, that all of you agree with one another in what you say and that there be no divisions among you, but that you be perfectly united in mind and thought. 1 Corinthians 1:10^{NIV}

DAILY RESTORATIONAL

Notes

Week 18

•••

Restore My Relationships

Above all, love each other deeply, because love covers a multitude of sins. 1 Peter 4:8^{NIV}

Often, we find ourselves in relationships that are unhealthy for us and our environments, however, we stay and cope. There are times when we have to navigate environments with people for whom we have mutual dislike. Nevertheless, we need to understand that people differ in values, opinions, ideas, and thoughts. Therefore, we should ask God to give us the tolerance, flexibility, and love to work, worship, or live with such persons.

Further, some people would sacrifice their lives for us, but we find ways to sabotage the relationship and push them away. However, some individuals voluntarily leave our lives and follow their own agendas. Perhaps, they realize they cannot manipulate us or dictate our lives for their gain. Jealousy could also play a large role in the termination of some relationships.

Does the following scenario sound familiar? You were drawn to an individual with whom you were incredibly compatible. Unfortunately, with time, things went array. The communication grew more awkward; the visits occurred less frequently, and the relationship became estranged. In the end, no one could explain what went wrong.

In addition, we must consider a third party's interference. It's possible that your relationship may have been disrupted by powers, rulers of darkness, principalities, or spiritual wickedness in high places. Living in harmony is an honor to God and signifies strength and unity for us in times of need, which indicates defeat for the enemy. Therefore, he will do whatever it takes to distract our minds from the people who, genuinely, love us and are willing to accept us for who we are. Satan may send his demons to whisper negative thoughts in your ears about your friends or family members. He may use false prophets or seers who are influenced by the spirit of divination to speak lies about the person you respect and love dearly. Thus, you believe the lies as truth and resent and withdraw from that individual. *Beloved, believe not every spirit, but try the spirits whether they are of God: because many false prophets are gone out into the world. 1 John 4:1*^{KJV}

Beloved, to rebuild your relationships, you must first build a relationship with God the Father, Jesus Christ the Son, and the Holy Spirit. There is one God who operates in three different offices. Jesus always intercedes and pleads for God's mercy on your behalf. Therefore, get connected and be sensitive to the Holy Spirit so you can hear His instructions and follow His directions to rebuild your earthly relationships.

Do not succumb to the idea that you can live without people and you don't need friends. The devil is a liar, and he wants you isolated so he can bombard you with the spirits of depression, oppression, frustration, and confusion. Before you know it, he will try to take full possession of you and introduce the spirit of suicide. God could have left Adam to be alone with the animals, but what would he do when his day's work was done? Could the animals respond to him? Could he seek their advice for his problems? If he fell ill, could the animals assist him? God witnessed Adam's circumstance and saw it not fit for man to be alone.

"No man is an island; no man stands alone," is a well-known quote and is true, indeed. We are mutually dependent on one another; therefore, we need people. We need communication and affirmation. For the next seven (7) days, command the restoration of the relationship between you and _____. (Insert the name or names) In the process, ask God for the love, patience, and understanding to deal with people.

Remember, not everyone thinks the way you do, and they may not share the same values or views.

Prayer

Dear Heavenly Father,

I love You and appreciate You. I exalt You above everyone else. You are holy and righteous, and I celebrate You. Thank You for being my strength, my rock, my fortress, and my deliverer. You are God, in whom I put my trust. I glorify Your name in all the Earth.

Father, in the name of Jesus, please forgive me for the known and unknown sins I have committed. Wash me thoroughly, and cleanse me from all impurities, iniquities, and transgressions. Father, in the mighty name of Jesus, please fix my shortcomings. Help me to acknowledge when I have done wrong.

Father God, I am reminded in Your Word that if it is possible, I should be at peace with everyone. In the mighty name of Jesus, I ask that You restore all my broken relationships that were meant to be but were sabotaged by the hand of the enemy. El Gibbor, the mighty God, You said, that by myself, I can chase one thousand demons, but with another person, we will chase ten thousand. You said by myself, I will prevail, two persons will withstand, but a threefold cord is not easily broken. Adonai, Satan knows the power of two or more, therefore, he tries to turn my friends and family against me and then whispers in my ears that they don't love me and they are not my friends. Father God, we need each other for strength, encouragement, and companionship. Lord, let not the enemy cause me to isolate myself from my brothers and sisters but to be at peace with them as we foster a loving, sincere relationship

In the mighty name of Jesus, I use the weapon of praise and worship to pull down and destroy the stronghold of sabotage and lies, in Jesus' name. I bind up every interfering, foul spirit that has come to sever my relationship with the people who love and care for me. In the name of Jesus, I bind up every jealous, envious, malicious, and covetous spirit, that is trying to put a rift in my relationships. In the name of Jesus, I bind every whispering, lying spirit that is planting negative thoughts and beliefs in my mind. May the consuming fire of God consume every evil work against my relationships. In the mighty name of Jesus, I break and destroy every curse and spell that was cast upon my relationships and the people with whom I am closely connected.

Jehovah Rophe, You are the Lord that heals. Thank You for healing and restoring my relationships, in Jesus' name. I declare that all my relationships are God-ordained and fruitful. Thank You that every hindrance to my relationships has been removed. Blessed be the Lord, forevermore! In Jesus' name, Amen.

But the Lord is faithful, who shall stablish you, and keep you from evil. 2 Thessalonians 3:3[KJV]

Notes

Week 19

⋯
Restore My Child(ren)'s Mind

But this is what the Lord says: "Yes, captives will be taken from warriors, and plunder retrieved from the fierce; I will contend with those who contend with you, and your children I will save.

Isaiah 49:25^{NIV}

Most parents are extremely proud of their child's accomplishments, while others worry for their children, daily. Despite your earnest efforts to raise your child respectably, sometimes circumstances are beyond your control, and your child grows into an individual you don't recognize, doing the opposite of what you taught them to do.

Perhaps your child is closely associated with peers who were a poor influence. As a result, your child's words and actions were negative. The harmful activities in which he or she engaged were embarrassing and kept you up at night.

Beloved, trust God with your child, and don't focus on what you see but on what God says. God understands your circumstance. Take your child's concerns and worries to Him and leave them on His altar. He will rectify the situation and keep you in perfect peace. As the earthly parent, who may still be raising children, be sure to train them with discipline and to have respect for both God and man. Do your best to share Christ with them as you emulate to them a Godly life. You have the power to declare restoration over your child. Don't give up on them.

Week 19 - Restore My Child(ren)'s Mind

Thirteen of the twenty-seven books in the New Testament were written by the Apostle Paul. Those books are known as "The Pauline Epistles" or the Epistle of Paul. Before his conversion and encounter with Jesus and the Holy Spirit, he was known as Saul of Tarsus, who knowingly persecuted Christians. He stood by and witnessed Christians get beaten and stoned to death and did nothing to stop the abuse. However, the same God who saved Saul and transformed him into Paul, an ambassador of Jesus Christ, can do the same for your child or children. If you take a closer look at your child, you will see the greatness which lies within him or her. Your child was born to positively impact lives. This is the reason why the fight against him or her is so intense. The enemy wants to ensure that your children do not fulfill their destiny.

Parents, I know you are hurting, and sometimes, you are tempted to say the wrong things to your children. Unfortunately, the words we heard from our parents growing up may still negatively affect us, today. Don't make the same mistakes your parents made and curse your progeny (descendant). Remember, death and life lie in the power of your tongue. Speak life and not death, blessings, and not curses. I encourage you to pray fervently. Be persistent in prayer on your child's behalf, and never cease your prayers. Today, I speak complete restoration into the life of your child. If you believe it, you will receive it.

> Be mindful of the negative words you speak over your children's lives. Think twice before you mistreat them. You never know, you may need them to take care of you in the future.

DAILY RESTORATIONAL

Prayer

Insert your child's or children's name in the blank spaces

Dear Heavenly Father,

Lord, I ask that you would restore_____'s mind.

Father God, You promised in Isaiah 54:13 that "All your sons will be taught by the LORD, and great will be your children's peace." Adonai, my Lord and Master, I plead the blood of Jesus over _____'s mind, soul, will, and emotions. I repent on behalf of _____'s sins to You. I call_____redeemed. Wrap _____in Your warm and loving arms and never let them go. I cancel every hindrance assigned to manipulate and distract _____ away from You.

May the fear of the Lord penetrate_____'s heart and spirit so Your angels can encamp around them, continuously. Master, as You kept a hedge around Job, please keep the same hedge of protection around_____. Keep a watch over _____ night and day. May nothing be lacking, missing, or broken from their life, in Jesus' name. Father God, as You have fed the birds of the air and clothed the lilies of the valley, continue to supply all_____'s needs according to Your riches in glory.

Jehovah Shalom, the God of peace, keep_____'s spirit in perfect peace. Thank You, Lord that _____ has the mind of Christ. I declare it to be sober, vigilant, focused, and God-fearing. Close every door in_____'s life that is not open by You.

Jehovah Rophe, You are the healer. Heal

Week 19 - Restore My Child(ren)'s Mind

_____'s heart, mind, soul, and spirit right now, in Jesus' name.

I rebuke every spirit of low self-esteem, inferiority, fear, self-hate, and inadequacy, in Jesus' Mighty name. I declare that _____'s identity and wholeness is found in You. Thank You for complete restoration of _____'s life, mind, body, soul, and spirit, in Jesus' name. Blessed be the Lord, forevermore! Amen.

Be grateful for the wholeness of your child's/children's mind.

DAILY RESTORATIONAL

Notes

Week 20

•••

Restore My Prayer Life

And pray in the Spirit on all occasions with all kinds of prayers and requests. With this in mind, be alert and always keep on praying for all the Lord's people. Ephesians 6:18^{NIV}

Given prayer that is one of the most effective weapons in the Christian arsenal, the enemy desires to completely destroy it. Prayer is such an essential part of our lives that the bible refers to it 375 times. Though the restoration and enhancement of their prayer life is often a goal, many people struggle with praying. Some individuals believe their prayers are boring, because they pray about the same things, continuously. Some are too timid to pray and think they can't do it, or they don't know how to and refuse to try. There are also individuals who do pray but lack anointing, power, fervency, and persistence. Satan's goal is to keep us ignorant of the power of prayer, for his major assignment is to oppose God's children and hinder us from walking in authority.

Has your prayer life experienced a dry spell? Your busy schedule interrupts you from seeking God's direction, as well as, your desire to spend time with Him. With the constant bustle of your day's assignments, you rarely make time in the morning or evening to engage the Holy Spirit and pray. When you do make time to pray, it is often interrupted by social media distractions and physical exhaustion.

Were you once an individual who continuously prayed and interceded for others? Were you the first to be called for prayer if someone was ill or had a tough decision to make? Do you recall the passion you once had as one of God's prayer warriors? Do you remember why and how you lost your zeal for prayer?

Beloved, there is no better time to restore your prayer life than right now, as the world needs much prayer. Perhaps you observed many situations that need to be addressed through prayer but feel as if you are not in the position to affect change because your prayer life has dwindled immensely. My friend, your prayer life can be restored if you condition your mind to deny social media distractions, decrease the length of time you spend watching television, and limit unnecessary phone conversations. You must be willing to create space and spend quality alone time with God. Ask Him to reveal to you any idols you may have in your life which have been given preeminence over Him.

Beloved, prayer provokes assistance from God and helps you navigate your path through life. Linger in His presence and re-cultivate a level of intimacy with Him again, and you will notice how your prayers can suspend demonic activities far and wide. Therefore, take an active role in fixing your problems, for God has given you power over the enemy. You possess more power than Satan and his demons, and you have been granted authority. Jesus gave you permission to use His name to cast out demons, if you believe. "And these signs shall follow them that believe; in my name shall they cast out devils; they shall speak with new tongues". Mark 16:17^{KJV}

The restoration of your prayer life will also require your commitment, consistency, and persistence. Beloved, this is not the time to retreat from or surrender your prayers. Your angels have been held hostage by principalities, powers, or spiritual wickedness in the heavens and need your persistent prayers to release them so you can receive your blessings and breakthrough. Therefore, pray without ceasing.

Mark 14:44 mentions that Jesus prayed the same words three times, so don't worry if you repeat your words while you pray. Challenge yourself with your prayers and remain consistent until change

Week 20 - Restore My Prayer Life

happens. The sixth chapter of Daniel demonstrates that Daniel prayed three times per day; and the 164th chapter of the book of Psalms indicates David prayed seven times a day. How many times will you commit to praying each day? The COVID-19 pandemic has shown us that we can find and make the time to do the things we've ignored over the years - given our preoccupation with other priorities.

Prayer is like a life vest; without it, you will drown.

Prayer

Dear Heavenly Father,

You are my refuge and my strength. You are my present help in the time of trouble. You are my rock, my shield, and my hiding place. Holy Spirit, I stand in awe of You. I lift up Your name on high, for all power belongs to You, O God. I pay homage to You, King of Kings and Lord of Lords.

Lord, I repent for all my transgressions and iniquities. Cleanse me, O God, from unrighteousness and purge me from all impurities. Lord, You have seen my thoughts and observed my actions, concerning prayer. I know my attitude towards prayer displeases You. Please forgive me. I confess that when I stopped praying, my life became shambles. Jehovah Shammah, You are always present, even when I walked away from our most excellent means of communication. Please forgive me for allowing my prayer life to be weakened. I realize that prayerlessness has opened doors, which allows the enemy to afflict my body, manipulate my mind, distort my personality, and, negatively, rearrange my attitude. Forgive me for taking the power of prayer lightly and for neglecting to spend time with You in prayer.

In the mighty name of Jesus, I use the weapon of prayer, praise, and worship to pull down and destroy every stronghold that rises up against my prayer life. Abba Father, I ask that You restore my hunger to pray without ceasing. In the name of Jesus, I command the restoration of my zeal to pray and intercede for others. Oh mighty God, restore my enthusiasm to prayer on the prayer-watch. In the name of Jesus, I command my soul to be watered with the effectual fervent prayer. In the name of Jesus, may my heart be filled with Your words so I can pray effectively. Mighty God, as the deer pants for the water so I long to communicate with You through prayer. Lord, I long to hear Your voice and to fellowship with You, through prayer. in Jesus' name.

El Haggdol, great God, I know the effectual fervent prayer of the righteous man avails much. Help me to pray always and without ceasing. O God of my salvation, El Yeshuati, in the name of Jesus, give me the unction to pray at least four times a day. In the mighty name of Jesus, give me the desire to pray and intercede for my community, country, and nations. Lord, as of today, I will be prayerful about every situation.

Thank You for preserving my prayer life. Thank You for keeping me hidden in Your secret place, in Jesus' name. Blessed be the Lord, forevermore! Amen.

Praying always with all prayer and supplication in the Spirit, and watching thereunto with all perseverance and supplication for all saints. Ephesians 6:18^{KJV}

Notes

Week 21

•••

RESTORE MY PRAYER LIFE

That if thou shalt confess with thy mouth the Lord Jesus, and shalt believe in thine heart that God hath raised him from the dead, thou shalt be saved. Romans 10:9^{KJV}

One source defines salvation as deliverance from sin and its consequences, as it is received by faith, in Christ. However, I believe salvation encompasses accepting and confessing with your mouth that Jesus Christ is Lord and Savior and acknowledging that His redemptive power saves us through His blood. We are most grateful to Jesus Christ because He offered His life as a ransom to preserve our own. This gift redeemed us from sin, spiritual death, and eternal damnation. We appreciate Him leaving the courts of glory to reconcile us unto Himself, so we may have the freedom to live forever, eternally.

Contrary to popular belief, becoming saved once does not guarantee one will always be saved. People have sacrificed their salvation because of money, sex, weariness, and other worldly positions and possessions. One cannot expect to regularly indulge in an ungodly lifestyle, frequently practice actions forbidden by God, fake holy behavior on the Sabbath and Sundays, and expect to enter the gates of heaven. Matthew 15:8^{KJV} reminds us, "This people draweth nigh unto me with their mouth, and honoureth me with their lips; but their heart is far from me." Matthew 7:21^{KJV} also declares, "Not everyone that saith unto me, Lord, Lord, shall enter into the kingdom of heaven; but he that doeth the will of my Father which is in heaven." Therefore, attending church services regularly and "acting holy" does not guarantee eternal salvation. God requires holiness, sanctification, and abstinence from sin to remain saved and free from bondage.

For instance, no one will be accepted as or remain a student at the University of the West Indies (UWI), Harvard, Princeton, or Yale University unless the exceptionally required admissions criteria are met. If those criteria are met for initial acceptance, a specific grade point average must be maintained to remain a student at that institution. Likewise, God has a notable standard we must cultivate to maintain our salvation and enter His kingdom. This is regardless of the leadership under which we were baptized or the church we attend. It is improper for believers to participate in worldly activities, such as going to clubs, partying, smoking, drinking, gambling, and contributing to corrupt conversations with the unsaved and unbelievers while expecting that God will honor that behavior and identify the believer as a faithful servant. Salvation is characterized by a change of heart, behavior, and mind.

Salvation is for everyone. However, not everyone will choose to accept it. Believers who uncuffed themselves from the world and sacrificed certain enjoyments should not compromise their character or integrity to avoid criticism from unbelievers. Conversely, has the world ever tried to do what the church does to escape judgment? Most unbelievers presume that salvation is for feeble-minded individuals. They enjoy their lives and consider submission to Christ as a sign of weakness which should only be explored as a last resort to depleted mental and physical strength. Why do we need Jesus and His salvation? With both, we are kept out of Hell, and we are protected from the wrath of Satan and his agents. Jesus and His salvation further prevent us from dying an eternal death without spiritual insurance and an eternal lifeline. Lastly, we need salvation to remain connected to God and not be separated from Him.

Beloved, salvation is still free; it's not up for time-sharing. Do not lower God's standards or expectation of you to satisfy your flesh or please your friends and family. Ultimately, your walk with God is a personal affair. The salvation of God requires us to live holy, be pure in mind, body, and spirit, and stay sanctified. Fulfilling anything other than the required standard of God is considered putting your hand to the plow and withdrawing it, which is referred to as backsliding. Jesus replied, *"No one who puts a hand to the plow and looks back is fit for service in the kingdom of God." Luke 9:62*[NIV]

Now is not the time to send your salvation on vacation. I hope your belief does not declare that the bible is a fictional book, and that, the second coming of Jesus Christ is a hoax, or that there is no Heaven or Hell. Beloved, death is inevitable. We will all die, but dying without Christ will be worse, because death does not end the life cycle. Death is followed by the judgment; and after the judgment, it will be revealed where you will spend eternity. [43] *And if thy hand offend thee, cut it off: it is better for thee to enter into life maimed, than having two hands to go into hell, into the fire that never shall be quenched:* [44] **Where their worm dieth not, and the fire is not quenched** Mark 9:43-44.

If you continue to reject God's invitation to build a relationship with Him or to accept Jesus Christ as your Lord and Savior, while you are alive, what do you expect Him to do for You after you die? Unfortunately, rejection of the salvation and the Savior will qualify you for a place that is prepared for Satan and his angels. It is a place where the worms do not die, and the fire burns, continuously. Nothing or no one is worth you losing your soul. You are valuable to God, which is the reason He gave up His life so you would not lose yours. He does not want you to face everlasting punishment and eternal torment. In this place, you will be begging to die but cannot die. Hell's fury is incomparable. What will your choice be? *Now we exhort you, brethren, warn them that are unruly, comfort the feebleminded, support the weak, be patient toward all men. 1 Thessalonians 5:14*[KJV]

Make a positive choice; God will make the changes.

Below are some bible verses confirming what is written above:

But whosoever shall deny me before men, him will I also deny before my Father which is in heaven. Matthew 10:33^{KJV}

And if thy hand offend thee, cut it off: it is better for thee to enter into life maimed, than having two hands to go into hell, into the fire that never shall be quenched: ⁴⁴Where their worm dieth not, and the fire is not quenched. Mark 9:43-44^{KJV}

Behold, I stand at the door, and knock: if any man hear my voice, and open the door, I will come in to him, and will sup with him, and he with me. Revelation 3:20^{KJV}

Whoever remains stiff-necked after many rebukes will suddenly be destroyed – without remedy. Proverbs 29:1^{NIV}

Then shall he say also unto them on the left hand, Depart from me, ye cursed, into everlasting fire, prepared for the devil and his angels. Matthew 25:41^{KJV}

For then must he often have suffered since the foundation of the world: but now once in the end of the world hath he appeared to put away sin by the sacrifice of himself. ²⁷ And as it is appointed unto men once to die, but after this the judgment: ²⁸ So Christ was once offered to bear the sins of many; and unto them that look for him shall he appear the second time without sin unto salvation. Hebrews 9:26-28^{KJV}

That if thou shalt confess with thy mouth the Lord Jesus, and shalt believe in thine heart that God hath raised him from the dead, thou shalt be saved. 10 For with the heart man believeth unto righteousness; and with the mouth confession is made unto salvation. Romans 10:9-10^{KJV}

Verily, verily, I say unto you, He that heareth my word, and believeth on him that sent me, hath everlasting life, and shall not come into condemnation; but is passed from death unto life. John 5:24^{KJV}

Neither is there salvation in any other: for there is none other name under heaven given among men, whereby we must be saved. Acts 4:12^{KJV}

Luke 16:23-28KJV

[23] And in hell he lift up his eyes, being in torments, and seeth Abraham afar off, and Lazarus in his bosom.

[24] And he cried and said, Father Abraham, have mercy on me, and send Lazarus, that he may dip the tip of his finger in water, and cool my tongue; for I am tormented in this flame.

[25] But Abraham said, Son, remember that thou in thy lifetime receivedst thy good things, and likewise Lazarus evil things: but now he is comforted, and thou art tormented.

[26] And beside all this, between us and you there is a great gulf fixed: so that they which would pass from hence to you cannot; neither can they pass to us, that would come from thence.

[27] Then he said, I pray thee therefore, father, that thou wouldest send him to my father's house:

[28] For I have five brethren; that he may testify unto them, lest they also come into this place of torment.

Prayer

Dear Heavenly Father,

Thank You for being awesome in my life. Thank You for Your gift of salvation.

Lord, I confess that I walked away from our relationship because of disobedience, doubt, and ungratefulness. Almighty God, I repent and ask for Your forgiveness for every sin I committed, whether by words, thoughts, or deeds. Please forgive me.

O Mighty God, if salvation was for sale I would not be able to buy it; so, thank You for sending Your Son to die in my place. Abba Father, thank You for purchasing my salvation with Your blood. Thank You, Jesus, for giving Your life as a ransom for my life so that I could inherit the kingdom of God through Your salvation plan. El Gibbor, mighty God, I believe in my heart and confess with my mouth, that Jesus Christ is Lord and He died on the cross for my sins, was buried, arose, and today, He is alive in my heart. Abba Father, I make the decision, today, to accept Your salvation and follow the teaching fundamentals of Your Word.

Abba Father, thank You for loving me. Thank You for restoring unto me the joy of my salvation, O glory to God. Lord, thank You for delivering me from the vice grip of the enemy, through Your plan of salvation, in Jesus mighty name. O Sovereign God, I recognize that Your amazing grace was granted to help transform my mind, body, and spirit. O God, revive me and help me to enjoy my salvation once again, in Jesus' name.

In the name of Jesus, I declare that I am made free through the blood of Jesus Christ of Nazareth, unto salvation. Blessed be the Lord, forevermore! Amen.

Be it known unto you all, and to all the people of Israel, that by the name of Jesus Christ of Nazareth, whom ye crucified, whom God raised from the dead, even by him doth this man stand here before you whole. Neither is there salvation in any other: for there is none other name under heaven given among men, whereby we must be saved. Acts 4:10, 12^{KJV}

Daily Restorational

Notes

Week 22

•••

RESTORE MY FEAR FOR GOD

Ye shall walk after the Lord your God, and fear him, and keep his commandments, and obey his voice, and ye shall serve him, and cleave unto him. Deuteronomy 13:4^{KJV}

Who is God to you? Is He someone you position on the sidelines, who you only call on when you need back-up? Is He your 911 responder only when you have an emergency? Or is He just someone you talk about, occasionally, without fear? The world has no fear or respect for God and His instructions, nor does the world esteem Him in high regard. Disappointingly, many consider Him a thorn in their flesh, because He will not agree or tolerate their iniquities or transgressions. Unless they turn from their rebellious and disrespectful ways, they will suffer the consequences of their behavior.

There is none that understandeth, there is none that seeketh after God. ¹²They are all gone out of the way, they are together become unprofitable; there is none that doeth good, no, not one. ¹³Their throat is an open sepulchre; with their tongues they have used deceit; the poison of asps is under their lips: ¹⁴Whose mouth is full of cursing and bitterness: ¹⁵Their feet are swift to shed blood: 16 Destruction and misery are in their ways: ¹⁷And the way of peace have they not known: ¹⁸**There is no fear of God before their eyes. Romans 3:11-18**^{KJV}

Fearing God does not mean being afraid of Him. Instead, having a fear of God demonstrates immense respect for Him and His Word.

Seek to be still in His presence, displaying reverence, honor, and high regard for His deity. The fear of God will move you to fall in love with Him and increase your desire to cease sinful behavior. If sinful behavior arises, your respect and reverence for God will make you repent, immediately. The fear of God will make you eager to please and exalt Him.

Beloved, Proverbs 9:10^{KJV} tells us that "the fear of the Lord is the beginning of wisdom: and the knowledge of the holy is understanding." I pray you have not lost your fear for God. If you have, I command it to be restored unto you right now, in Jesus' name. The fear of God will provide wisdom and insight. Without this fear, nothing else will matter. Seek the wisdom of God, and be obedient, as the alternative will incite disconnection in your relationship with God. I encourage you to return to your first love-the agape love. When your love and fear for God is activated, the odds of you participating comfortably in any ungodly act is less likely. Yield yourself completely into His mighty hands, and surrender your thoughts and mind to Him, today.

Let us hear the conclusion of the whole matter: Fear God, and keep his commandments: for this is the whole duty of man. Ecclesiastes 12:13^{KJV}

Twenty Amazing Benefits For Those Who "Fear" the Lord, found in Psalm 112:1-10^{KJV}

1. You will gain divine wisdom.
2. You will have an excellent relationship with God.
3. He will call you friend.
4. You, your children, and your grandchildren will be blessed.
5. You will be protected.
6. Your children will be mighty.
7. Wealth and riches will be your portion.

8. You will walk in favor.
9. You will receive His grace and mercy.
10. Your path will be clear, despite the darkness.
11. Righteousness will be yours, forever
12. You will be guided and directed.
13. No one or nothing will move you.
14. You will always be remembered.
15. You will not be afraid of evil.
16. Your heart will cling to God.
17. You will trust God.
18. You will see your desire upon the wicked.
19. God will destroy your enemies and the wickedness which rises against you.
20. You will keep His commandments.

Prayer

Dear Heavenly Father,

I will praise You, with every breath I take. I will praise You with my whole heart. My soul magnifies You, my mouth blesses You, and my spirit worships You. Sovereign King, I will forever exalt Your marvelous works. Thank You, Lord, for Your grace and mercy.

Abba Father, I know I sinned against You when I lost the fear for God. Please forgive me. Master, I acknowledge my weaknesses and vulnerability; and I admit that I have disrespected and dishonored You and Your Word. Please forgive me. Father God, I realize that without my fear for You, my life is out of control. Forgive me for not acknowledging Your sovereignty and showing respect to You. Lord, I surrender to You and turn from my sins, in Jesus' mighty name.

O Father God, I am reminded in Ecclesiastes 12:13 that I should fear You and keep Your commandments because it is the whole duty of man. Mighty God, in the name of Jesus, grant me the wisdom to fear You, for as it is written that fearing God is the beginning of wisdom.

In the mighty name of Jesus Christ, I denounce, renounce, and reject anything that has caused me to lose the fear of God. God of righteousness, in the mighty name of Jesus, I ask that You restore my fear and reverence for You so I may talk right, walk right, think right, and live right. Father, as of today, I will trust and follow You as my Jehovah Hoshe'ah, the Lord who saves. Hallelujah.

I use the weapon of faith and boldness to destroy the stronghold of fear, in Jesus' name. Holy Spirit, I thank You for restoring the fear for God in my life, in Jesus' name. Blessed be the Lord, forevermore! Amen.

I acknowledged my sin unto thee, and mine iniquity have I not hid. I said, I will confess my transgressions unto the LORD; and thou forgavest the iniquity of my sin. Psalm 32:5[KJV]

Week 23

RESTORE MY LOVE

Though I speak with the tongues of men and of angels, and have not charity, I am become as sounding brass, or a tinkling cymbal. ²And though I have the gift of prophecy, and understand all mysteries, and all knowledge; and though I have all faith so that I could remove mountains, and have not charity, I am nothing. ³And though I bestow all my goods to feed the poor, and though I give my body to be burned, and have not charity, it profiteth me nothing. ⁴Charity suffereth long, and is kind; charity envieth not; charity vaunteth not itself, is not puffed up,⁵ Doth not behave itself unseemly, seeketh not her own, is not easily provoked, thinketh no evil.

1 Corinthians 13:1-4^{KJV}

Authentic love is the most fascinating emotion. Studies attest that there are eight different types of love. However, most people generally make reference to only three: Philia/ Philos, Eros, and Agape. Philia/ Philos refers to casual friendship; Eros describes an intimate relationship between a man and a woman; and Agape expresses an unconditional affection with no limits or conditions. Agape describes the spiritual love we receive from God, our Father. Which love are you missing?

Are you struggling to find love in your heart for God or someone else? For whom did your love grow cold? Some people know how best to agitate you, but understand that they are used as a tool of Satan to make you transgress against God and lose your salvation. Knowing that God is love, you should exert an earnest effort to express real love to those who deliberately hurt you. It is impossible for you to have hatred for man and love for God in the same heart.

Matthew 5:23-24^{NIV} reminds us, *Therefore, if you are offering your gift at the altar and there remember that your brother or sister has something against you, ²⁴leave your gift there in front of the altar. First, go and be reconciled to them; then come and offer your gift.*

Beloved, it is not easy to love those who hurt us, but, if you want to make heaven your final home, you must ask God to remove your hardened heart and replace it with a heart filled with forgiveness, love, and compassion. For instance, in marriage, you must be honest with your spouse to keep the marriage strong and healthy.

You both should continue to date each other, travel, and maintain spontaneity. Your love should not grow cold for one another. If you can always look at your spouse with the same admiration and enthusiasm as when you first met and through the eyes of God, your love will get stronger over time. It is not impossible to keep your marriage strong, if it was ordained by God. When you genuinely love someone, you will forgive their mistakes and rectify things with them because that is an expectation of God. Do not allow yourself to be taken advantage of, but when you let the love of God permeate your heart, you will still care, admire, and show respect to the person, despite their behavior. You will balance the other person and complement what they lack.

> Sincere love doesn't take revenge, think about evil, keep malice, or harbor resentment.

Prayer

Dear Heavenly Father,

You are my Shield and Buckler. Thank You for being Jehovah Yish'ie, the horn of my salvation, and I will forever praise You. Thank You for being the rock of my salvation. Lord, I exalt You and lift Your name on high.

Father, I humbly bow before You today, asking You to forgive me for every sin that I committed. Forgive me for allowing my love for You and others to grow cold. Father God, in the mighty name of Jesus, please forgive me for speaking negatively against my sisters and brothers. Jehovah Tsidkenu, God of righteousness, my heart is holding onto grudge, anger, unforgiveness, and malice. In the name of Jesus, please forgive me and cleanse me of all my iniquities. In the mighty name of Jesus, I seek Your forgiveness for the continuous brewing of evil thoughts in my mind, and the harboring of hatred in my heart. Father God, I transgressed against You, trespassed against others, and committed iniquity in my heart, please forgive me. O, mighty God, I know that I cannot have hatred in my heart and still profess to be a real, born-again believer. Psalm 66: 18 reminds me that if I regard iniquity in my heart, You will not hear me when I pray. Purify my heart O God.

In the name of Jesus, I use the weapon of love to destroy the stronghold of hate, in Jesus' name. I command my spirit-man to line up with 1 Corinthians 13. Lord, help me to be sincere when I speak and exhibit love to everyone, regardless of their indifferences, in Jesus' name. Help me, Father, not become sounding brass or a noisy cymbal. In the mighty name of Jesus, I command pure love to flow out of my heart so that my gift of prophecy, knowledge, and understanding will not come to naught.

Because of the restoration of the agape love, my feeding of the poor and my sacrifices will not be in vain. In the mighty name of Jesus, I will not envy anyone. In the mighty name of Jesus, I will not boast;

and I will not be self-seeking. O, mighty God, thank You for restoring the kind of love that restrains me from behaving out of character, thinking evil, rejoicing in iniquity or over any ones' mishap.

Jehovah Mephalti, Lord my deliverer, thank You for delivering me from the spirit of hate, in Jesus' name. Thank You for restoring the love that never fails. Thank You for restoring the love that beareth all things, believeth all things, hopeth all things, endureth all things. Thank You for restoring the spirit of love within me so I can sincerely love my enemies, bless them who curse me, do good to them who hate me, and pray for them who despitefully use and persecute me, in Jesus' name. Help me to love without any conditions or limitations. Thank You for restoring my love for You and others. Blessed be the Lord, forevermore! Amen and Amen.

If a man says, "I love God," and hateth his brother, he is a liar. For he that loveth not his brother whom he hath seen, how can he love God whom he hath not seen? 1 John 4:20^{KJV}

Notes

Week 24

•••

RESTORE MY DISCERNMENT

And this is my prayer: that your love may abound more and more in knowledge and depth of insight, ¹⁰so that you may be able to discern what is best and may be pure and blameless for the day of Christ.
Philippians 1:9-10 NIV

I have a friend who wrote a book titled, *When Satan Went to Church*. My attention was immediately arrested by the title. I found it appropriate, given he does attend church, sometimes unidentified and under disguise. Satan and his agents attend church regularly, to carry out wicked assignments against the children of God. Unfortunately, without the spirit of discernment, one can be easily deceived by mistaking demons for the deacons, shaking hands with witches, mistaking them for the ushers, and confiding in warlocks, believing them to be the pastor of the true and living God. Satan's goal is to distract and spiritually paralyze the saints of God, causing them to fall from grace and lose their salvation.

Perhaps you were fooled by Satan's disguises when his agent approached you with the offer to become your prayer partner and engaged you in bible studies. However, with time, you sensed a different agenda and noticed a higher level of vulnerability towards this individual, which weakened your desire for the things of God. Sadly, your lack of spiritual discernment caused you to ignore those warning signs, as a result, you were left facing the consequences.

Beloved, the gift of discernment is given by God as a form of protection, because He doesn't want any of His followers to be

Week 24 - Restore My Discernment

blind or unaware. You should be able to recognize and discern the intention of the enemy and intercept their plans. Restoring your spirit of discernment requires spending quality time with God. It is important to read His Word and meditate on it day and night. Studying and memorizing the Word will give you an insight into the heart and plans of God. He will reveal to you what you need to see and understand. Like Joseph, Jesus, and Moses, you were targeted because of the greatness inside you. A greatness that, once exposed, will re-arrange lives, change hearts, and save souls. This greatness is the reason Satan tried to compromise your discernment and leave you spiritually blind. Nonetheless, this race is not a sprint but a marathon; you are in it for the long haul. Along the journey, you will face obstacles, get weary, and may fall numerous times. However, I encourage you to get up, brush yourself off, refuel, and command the spirit of discernment to be your armor.

Prayer

Dear Heavenly Father,

I will bless You Lord, oh my soul, and forget not Your benefits. Lord Jesus, You are the lover of my soul, and there is none that compares to You. Lord, I thank You for Your mercies toward me. Thank You for loving me, unconditionally. God, I give You glory and praise. My Master and King, I celebrate the works of Your hands. Lord, how excellent is Your name in all the Earth.

Jehovah Eli, the Lord my God. Even though I have hurt You numerous times, You kept forgiving me, loving me, and providing for me. Thank You, God, for Your unlimited mercy and Your amazing grace. Father, please forgive me for every sin I have committed. Hold me with Your right hand of righteousness, and lead me in a straight and narrow way. In Jesus' name.

Omnipotent Father, You know what is in the darkness. Nothing is hidden from You. In the name of Jesus, I command my discernment to be restored. Father, You said, there will be no secret that will not be revealed and anything hidden will be known and come to the light. Retrain my spiritual my eyes to discern the hidden and secret things, in Jesus' name. O, Mighty God, help me to discern the nets and the traps that the enemy has set for me, in Jesus' name. Open my eyes to see where they have hidden their snares and lay in wait for me. In the mighty name of Jesus, I will not perish because of a lack of discernment, in Jesus name.

Through the power of the Holy Ghost, I bind up every evil works and attack of the enemy against my spiritual and physical eyesight. In the name of Jesus, I cancel every assignment against my discernment. In the name of Jesus, I frustrate every ambush set up against me by my enemy. In the name of Jesus, I will not be taken off guard by the enemy. In the mighty name of Jesus, may their conspiracy come to naught.

Thank You, mighty God, for restoring my discernment to identify right from wrong, good from evil, and the Holy Spirit from the false and foul spirits. Almighty God, thank You for allowing my path to be like the morning sun. Thank You, God, for removing the scales from my eyes. Thank You for restoring my discernment. Blessed be the Lord, forevermore! In Jesus' name, Amen.

Dear friends, do not believe every spirit, but test the spirits to see whether they are from God, because many false prophets have gone out into the world. 1 John 4:1^{NIV}

Notes

Week 25

•••

RESTORE THE SPIRIT OF EXCELLENCE

Then this Daniel was preferred above the presidents and princes, because an excellent spirit was in him; and the king thought to set him over the whole realm. Daniel 6:3^{KJV}

Even though people speak about and may desire excellence, many fall short of doing what it takes to be excellent. Excellence involves striving to be and do our best at all times, regardless of the obstacles, which try to throw us off course. The spirit of excellence won't allow us to take short-cuts but will require us to go the extra mile to complete a particular assignment. When we embrace greatness and brilliance, we will not settle for mediocrity. The more we intensify our search for excellence, the more distinguished we will become.

We serve a superior God whose character and integrity are laced with excellence. If we are His heirs, we should desire excellence as well. Choosing to do the right thing when no one is looking or cheering us on is an expression of the spirit of excellence. The spirit of excellence is also evident when we willingly become servants-serving others to the best of our abilities, and lending our time and presence without being paid or reimbursed.

Perhaps, at one point in your life, you were incredibly meticulous about what you did, or the way you looked or the way you spoke. You were very distinguished. However, now you find yourself exhibiting a careless attitude and a spirit of mediocrity. Things you wouldn't usually do or participate in, now, seem to be your norm. Restoring the spirit of excellence will propel you to do the right thing, even when the flesh rebels, and you are alone with no one watching. The spirit of excellence should be present in the absence of an audience.

Beloved, possessing an excellent spirit comes only through allowing God to be the CEO (Chief Executive Officer) of your life. With God being the center of your life, out of love and fear for Him, you will seek to do the right thing at all times. Like Daniel, onlookers will identify your superiority, brilliance, and your distinctive demeanor. Even people whom you don't know will be drawn to you and may choose you to oversee or operate their affairs above qualified people in authority. No matter what you have accomplished or how great you are, never stop excelling; continue to raise the bar for yourself. Michael Jordon could have said, "I am the best basketball player that has walked the earth, and I don't need to attend the practice games". However, he didn't. He showed up for every practice and went above and beyond to maintain his excellent basketball skills. He made room for improvement and growth; and he excelled.

God does care about how you handle your daily affairs and your secular business. Ultimately, He is the one who provides it for you. Therefore, He expects you to be good stewards of your earthly possessions. It would be a wise idea to keep company with those whose excellence you admire; and connect with those who have shared your goals, especially if you are a business owner. Delivering excellence to your clients should be a priority in your core values. Pay attention to details and what they care about; and make sure they are satisfied, happy, and comfortable. *He that walketh with wise men shall be wise: but a companion of fools shall be destroyed. Proverbs 13:20*^{KJV}

Beloved, be yourself and never compare your excellence to someone else's. There will always be someone with a stronger skill set. Perhaps you compare yourself to those who have been consistently working to improve their excellence for many years. Be the best person you can be; and continue to strive for excellence. Possessing the spirit of excellence will not happen instantly, but when you make it a habit, you will find there is always room for improvement and adjustment, to cultivate a spirit of excellence. Be open and ready to embrace change.

What are some of the signs that you no longer possess the spirit of excellence?

This list is not exhaustive, but if you find yourself willfully compromising daily etiquette, disregarding details, or carelessly neglecting standards, you may be lacking the spirit of excellence.

If you find yourself doing some of the following, you may have lost your spirit of excellence:

- Consistently late for work, school, church or scheduled meetings
- Purposely leaving an item on the wrong shelf in the store or supermarket
- Insensitivity to people with disabilities. For instance, not being handicapped but still parking in the handicap space
- Throwing garbage through the car window while driving
- Neglecting to pay your bills on time, even though you are financially able
- Failure to pay for rendered services
- Failure to repay borrowed money
- Spitting loosely in public
- Failure to reverence God

These are a few examples of lacking the spirit of excellence. You may not have an answer or an explanation for the loss, but if you sincerely command its restoration, you can repossess it and walk with dignity.

Week 25 - Restore the Spirit of Excellence

After all, it is time for restoration. Finally, brothers, whatever is true, whatever is honorable, whatever is just, whatever is pure, whatever is lovely, whatever is commendable, if there is any excellence, if there is anything worthy of praise, think about these things. Philippians 4:8 KJV

Seest thou a man diligent in his business? he shall stand before kings; he shall not stand before mean men. Proverbs 22:29 KJV

> The spirit of excellence should be present in the absence of an audience.

Prayer

Dear Heavenly Father,

Thank You for being an Omniscient Father, mighty God of Zion. How excellent is Your name on the earth. Master, I celebrate You, and I bow before You in awe. Sweet rose of Sharon, Lily of the valley, I embrace Your awesomeness today. Praise Your name, Lord.

Search my heart O God, and uproot any trace of bitterness, anger, unforgiveness, or selfishness. Adonai, destroy any hint of pride found within me. O, mighty God, in the name of Jesus, I repent of every sin that is hindering me from getting closer to You. In the mighty name of Jesus, I repent of any sin that has prevented me from expressing the spirit of excellence.

In the mighty name of Jesus, I command the spirit of excellence to manifest through my heart, speech, walk, action, and thoughts. In the name of Jesus, I use the weapon of excellence to pull down and destroy the stronghold of mediocrity and complacency out of my life, in Jesu's name. Father God, I ask that You restore unto me the spirit of excellence. Help me, O God to represent You with excellence in everything that I do and say, in Jesus' mighty name. Elyon, the most high God, You are a God who does everything with decency and order. Help me to reflect Your character and express a spirit of excellence, in Jesus' name.

El Shaddai, the all-sufficient God, thank You for delivering me from the spirit of mediocrity and restoring the spirit of excellence. Thank You, Abba Father for helping me to be excellent in faith, knowledge, wisdom, and understanding. Thank You, Father God, that I can now express the spirit of excellence and do the right thing, even when there is no one around. Blessed be the Lord, forevermore! In Jesus' name, Amen.

But since you excel in everything – in faith, in speech, in knowledge, in complete earnestness and in the love we have kindled in you – see that you also excel in this grace of giving. 2 Corinthians 8:7 [NIV]

Week 25 - Restore the Spirit of Excellence

Notes

Week 26

•••

Restore a Servant's Heart

Just as the Son of Man did not come to be served, but to serve, and to give his life as a ransom for man. Matthew 20:28^{NIV}

Many individuals want to be recognized for their accomplishments. They will gladly tell you about their educational experiences, and without hesitation, are quick to tell you about their professions. Of course, they should be proud of their accomplishments and professional growth, as well as be acknowledged for their achievements.

However and unfortunately, no one wants to be known as or be called a servant. Often, servanthood is not viewed as sophisticated work. For most, being a servant seems degrading and demeaning, because those who serve are often looked down upon, given the work they do. However, acknowledging your calling to be a servant is one of the best gifts you can ever offer yourself and others.

Beloved, regardless of the title or position you hold, if you imagine yourself as a servant who offers a unique service, you may enjoy your life and career even more. In fact, you will feel more fulfilled because you can serve others in necessary capacities. Being a servant can be very rewarding, and it is one of the highest recognitions one can ever receive, and it does not require a college education. As a pastor, prophet, evangelist, or a miracle worker, never elevate yourself so highly in your role that you cannot serve in less glamorous areas of work. Exercising humility amidst accomplishment elicits the utmost respect. You were born to serve; therefore, ask God to restore your

Week 26 - Restore a Servant's Heart

servant's heart and attitude. According to 2 Timothy 2:24NIV And the Lord's servant must not be quarrelsome but must be kind to everyone, able to teach, not resentful.

12 When he had finished washing their feet, he put on his clothes and returned to his place. "Do you understand what I have done for you?" he asked them. 13 "You call me 'Teacher' and 'Lord,' and rightly so, for that is what I am. 14 Now that I, your Lord and Teacher, have washed your feet, you also should wash one another's feet. 15 I have set you an example that you should do as I have done for you. 16 Very truly I tell you, no servant is greater than his master, nor is a messenger greater than the one who sent him. 17 Now that you know these things, you will be blessed if you do them. John 13:12-17NIV

When you serve, you will be served.

Prayer

Dear Heavenly Father,

How marvelous are the works of Your hands. O sovereign God, the Creator of the Universe, You took nothing and created it into a beautiful world. All glory be to Your name, Lord, for You are magnificent, superb, and excellent. I praise Your name.

Jehovah, Mephalti, Lord my deliver, please deliver me from my pompous, stuck-up attitude. Forgive me for not walking in humility. Forgive me for my selfish motives. Abba Father, forgive me for any sin that is preventing me from becoming the servant You created me to be.

In the mighty name of Jesus, with the weapon of humility, I pull down and destroy the stronghold of pride and any other sin that is preventing me from exhibiting a servant's heart, in Jesus' mighty name. Jehovah Goe'l, my redeemer, please restore unto me the desire for service and the heart to serve, in Jesus' name. Father God, help me to follow Your great example of being a servant, in Jesus' name.

Lord, I acknowledge that I am a servant, one who was sent to earth to serve others, unconditionally, in Jesus' name. Lord, help me not to think that I am better than serving the less fortunate but serve everyone with great humility, compassion, and enthusiasm. Father, in the name of Jesus, help me to serve with pure motives and good intentions. Jehovah Bara, You have blessed me to be a blessing, let me not be stingy with it, in Jesus' name.

Today, I declare that I will serve, faithfully. Thank You for restoring my servant's heart. Blessed be the Lord, forevermore! In Jesus' name, Amen.

But you are not to be like that. Instead, the greatest among you should be like the youngest, and the one who rules like the one who serves.
Luke 22:26^{NIV}

Week 26 - Restore a Servant's Heart

Notes

Week 27

...

RESTORE MY OBEDIENCE

Know ye not, that to whom ye yield yourselves servants to obey, his servants ye are to whom ye obey; whether of sin unto death, or of obedience unto righteousness? Romans 6:16 KJV

Have you ever considered how quickly we obey the commands of man over the commands and direction of God? For instance, the entire world obeyed man's orders to shut their businesses down, close the doors of the church, stay home, wear masks and gloves, and avoid large gatherings. There was no retaliation, no questions asked, and no rebelling, and the majority of individuals obeyed- and rightly so. Our heavenly father told us to obey the law of the land. As this pandemic prolongs, men seek out the government for solutions, comfort, and reassurance, while still obeying their orders. Some individuals want to make sure they have not been affected by COVID-19. They line up to get tested, as they were encouraged to do; but what they really wanted is reassurance that they are safe, protected, and won't die.

Perhaps, if you were as obedient to the voice of God, you would avoid living in turmoil and be spared the heartache from that relationship or avoid a bitter divorce. With obedience, you could avoid foreclosure on your home, repossession of your vehicle, or mountainous debt. It is also a possibility that if you were obedient, you would not be suffering from that particular disease or illness. Overall, many mishaps in our lives could have been prevented, if we had only listened and obeyed God's instructions and warnings.

Week 27 - Restore My Obedience

Beloved, disobedience is a choice. If you have been committing the sin of disobedience, it is not too late to turn things around on the path of obedience. When God says "Let thy kingdom come on earth as it is in heaven" or "seek ye first the kingdom of God and His righteousness", He is saying: seek my principles. Stick to my rule and authority. Use my system to get things done. Apply my discipline to your life. Adopt my way of being organized. God compares the sin of disobedience to witchcraft. Make a U-turn into the arms of God, and rebuild a sincere relationship with Him.

God will not overlook your disobedience in one area because you were faithful in most areas. Can you identify in which area you are disobedient? Adam and Eve may have obeyed everything else except the eating from the forbidden tree, but it still cost them their freedom and inheritance. Please, listen attentively to His voice, and consider which commandment you have disobeyed, and repent.

All his commandments are still valid today; He is expecting us to obey them. Will you slip and fall? Yes, but once you get up and ask for forgiveness, God will grant it. Disobedience can be classified as presumptuous sin, which God will not tolerate. Choose to do what God asked of you without doubting, questioning, or rebelling. God is fair, loving, and compassionate, but He is a God of discipline and order. His commissions and commandments are mandatory, don't allow yourself to suffer the consequences. The following scripture, taken from Revelation 2:13-16 NIV, was a message to one of the seven churches: I know where you live—where Satan has his throne. Yet you remain true to my name. You did not renounce your faith in me, not even in the days of Antipas, my faithful witness, who was put to death in your city—where Satan lives.[14]Nevertheless, I have a few things against you: There are some among you who hold to the teaching of Balaam, who taught Balak to entice the Israelites to sin so that they ate food sacrificed to idols and committed sexual immorality. [15] Likewise, you also have those who hold to the teaching of the Nicolaitans. [16] Repent therefore! Otherwise, I will soon come to you and will fight against them with the sword of my mouth.

[19]Therefore anyone who sets aside one of the least of these commands and teaches others accordingly will be called least in the kingdom of heaven, but whoever practices and teaches these commands will be called great in the kingdom of heaven. [20] For I tell you that unless your righteousness surpasses that of the Pharisees and the teachers of the law, you will certainly not enter the kingdom of heaven. Matthew 5:19-20[NIV]

And they will go out and look on the dead bodies of those who rebelled against me; the worms that eat them will not die, the fire that burns them will not be quenched, and they will be loathsome to all mankind. Isaiah 66:24[NIV]

Obedience is an act of worship. Obedience proves our love for God. Obedience demonstrates our faith in God. God rewards obedience. The penalty for disobedience is death. What will you choose?

Prayer

Dear Heavenly Father,

I appreciate You. I love and adore You, and I bow down before You. Holy Spirit, I appreciate You. Lord, You are wonderful, sweet, and precious. Jesus, You are so beautiful. You are magnificent, and I celebrate Your majesty.

Jehovah, in the name of Jesus, I repent for being disobedient. Because of my disobedience, I have been spiritually, physically, and financially stagnant. My inheritance is delayed, and reaching my full potential in You has been hindered. Forgive me, O God.

In the mighty name of Jesus, I use the weapon of obedience to pull down the stronghold of disobedience. Through the power, in the name of Jesus, I cast down all imaginations and every high thing that exalts itself against the knowledge of God; and I bring into captivity

Week 27 - Restore My Obedience

every negative, disobedient thought to the obedience of Jesus Christ. In the name of Jesus, I am ready to revenge all disobedience as my obedience is fulfilled in Christ.

Elohim, I ask that You restore my obedience. Help me to obey Your every Word and continue to walk in obedience and apply Your instructions. Lord, remove the spirit of rebellion and pride that is causing me to disobey You. Father God, I purpose in my heart to walk in obedience.

As of today, I declare that I will no longer yield my obedience to the adversary. Spirit of disobedience, I bind up your works and assignment against my obedience, in Jesus' name. Abba Father, help me to guard my heart against deception, as I walk in complete obedience to Your Word. By faith, I loose the spirit of obedience into my life. I loose the blessing, favor, protection, and fear of God upon me, in Jesus' name.

Thank You for restoring my obedience, in Jesus' name. Blessed be the Lord, forevermore! Amen.

If you are willing and obedient, you will eat the good things of the land; Isaiah 1:19[NIV]

DAILY RESTORATIONAL

Notes

Week 28

•••

RESTORE MY GRATITUDE

Being enriched in everything to all bountifulness, which causeth through us thanksgiving to God. For the administration of this service not only supplieth the want of the saints, but is abundant also by many thanksgivings unto God; 2 Corinthians 9:11-12^{KJV}

Gratitude has been defined as being strongly and consistently associated with greater happiness. Gratitude helps people feel more positive emotions, relish good experiences, improve their health, manage adversity, and build strong relationships.

The word gratitude derives from the Latin word "gratus", which means "thankful; pleasing." If you consider the journey of your life from birth until now and remember all the things God provided for you and protected you from, do you think you have thanked Him enough? Have you expressed an adequate amount of gratitude?

Have you considered the individuals who have heavily influenced your life? Have you ever stopped to let them know how they have positively impacted your life? You should make time to say, "thank you." If someone does something pleasing for you, tell them how they made you feel. Every opportunity you get, don't hesitate to show and tell your family and friends how grateful you are for them and how much they mean to you. They may be present one minute and gone the next. It is fulfilling to make someone's day by expressing your gratitude for them and watching their smile grow as they, in turn, express their gratitude for you.

Beloved, do not wait until an individual passes away to express your gratitude for them. Send them flowers, gifts, and food while they are still alive to appreciate and enjoy it. Express your love through action. Making expensive funeral arrangements, after a person dies, means far less than the time you missed or the help you didn't offer when they were alive. Determine today, that you will make a list of all the individuals who have made a difference in your life, and reach out to them. Put forth an earnest effort to spend quality time with your friends and loved ones.

Paul reminded us in 1Thessalonians 5:18 that, *In everything give thanks: for this is the will of God in Christ Jesus concerning you.* In other words, what you are experiencing may not feel good to the flesh, and you wish the situation was different but take the time to praise, pray, worship, and give thanks to God despite the hardship. You never know, by managing your challenges and choosing to be thankful, instead of murmuring and complaining, your situation may not seem so unbearable. Therefore, challenge yourself to practice gratitude. Think of five things for which you are thankful, and before you get out of bed in the morning, thank God for them. Throughout the day, express thankfulness to God for all things, including your food, your challenges, and your successes. Always give thanks.

I encourage you to maintain a moment-by-moment awareness of your thoughts, feelings, and surrounding environment and always be thankful. Keeping a gratitude journal could be helpful, as well.

Never forget to express an attitude of gratitude; be thankful.

Week 28 - Restore My Gratitude

Prayer

Dear Heavenly Father,

You are welcome in every part of my life. Holy Spirit, I honor and adore You. Thank You for being my mentor, my coach, and my inspiration. I love and respect Your faithfulness.

Adonai, You are my Lord and Master, please forgive me for being ungrateful. Your Word said that ungratefulness is worse than the sin of witchcraft. In the mighty name of Jesus, please uproot the spirit of ungratefulness out of me, O, God. Father God, forgive me for taking all that You do for me for granted. In the name of Jesus, I ask that You wash me, cleanse and purify me from all unrighteousness and the sin of ungratefulness.

Abba Father, Thank You for life, health, and strength. Thank You for sending Your angels to protect and encamp around me. Thank You, Lord, for the many blessings and favor You have poured down on me. Thank You, Master, for lifting a standard against the enemy when they come in like a flood. Thank You for being my refuge and strength. Lord, I thank You for being a shield for me and the lifter of my head. Almighty God, I praise You for the use of my limbs. I honor You for my family and the ability to provide for them.

In the name of Jesus, I use the weapon of gratitude and pull down and destroy the stronghold of ungratefulness. Adonai, In the name of Jesus, I ask that You restore my gratitude and help me not to lose it, again. Father, from this moment onward, I will practice and express an attitude of gratitude. Blessed be the Lord, forevermore! In Jesus' name, Amen.

I exhort therefore, that, first of all, supplications, prayers, intercessions, and giving of thanks, be made for all men; 1 Timothy 2:1^{KJV}

Daily Restorational

Notes

Week 29

•••

RESTORE MY PATIENCE

Be still before the Lord and wait patiently for him; do not fret when people succeed in their ways, when they carry out their wicked schemes. 8 Refrain from anger and turn from wrath; do not fret—it leads only to evil. 9 For those who are evil will be destroyed, but those who hope in the Lord will inherit the land. Psalm 37:7-9 NIV

We often say, "Lord give me patience," but later, we question the manifestation of a problem, a disappointment, or a delay. Be reminded that these things are not manifested to kill or hurt you, even though that is the desire of the enemy for your soul. Generally, problems, disappointments, and delays are a prerequisite for patience. Most times, we blame the devil when we face hurdles or challenges, not knowing that God may have allowed them for our own safety or protection. He may also be honoring our request for patience. We will always encounter adversities. The trials and struggles we face serve as spiritual development for God's purpose to be established in our lives. We may have been enduring hardship and turmoil for a long time, but it should be considered a process that we cannot bypass. Think of a piece of rib-eye steak. If you take it off the grill too soon, it will be undercooked. For us to develop patience, we must linger a little longer in the fire. The longer it takes for us to overcome our trials, the greater our endurance will be to face what's to come.

Patience does not develop overnight. It, too, cannot be bought, leased, rented, or sold. Patience is a virtue that grows from within through tests and trials. It is a requirement that we cannot pray away, but God promises to be with us until the very end. When patience manifests on the outside, it was inwardly cultivated over a long period of time. What we are going through now is a test run; for we are being trained and equipped to trust and exercise faith in God during the great tribulations that will be coming on Earth. If we refuse to endure the trials now when the world around us begins to crumble, so will we because we have no spiritual investment-no foundation, and no immunity. Our spiritual immune systems are compromised.

Beloved, Romans 5:3 states that "Tribulation worketh patience." Like going to the gym, keep exercising your patience. Beloved, even though you are experiencing tough times, don't focus on what you see. Don't allow it to distract you. Instead, draw closer to God, and activate your trust, faith, and belief in Him. Build a solid, unshakeable foundation by digging deeper into the Word of God. Find other like-minded individuals who will fast and pray with you, regularly, while you embrace your challenges. With joy, rejoice in your sufferings and celebrate the grace and mercy of God in your hardships, for hardship produces patience and endurance. Trials, pain, tribulation, difficulty, and lack may not be a bad thing, because they thrust you into the arms of God. They allow you to seek and depend upon Him and not man or self.

When your patience is lacking, it can cause you to be rude and disrespectful to others, and upset with God. Without patience, you will run ahead of God and make a mess of your life. The next time you get upset, when your plans don't follow through or when you were impulsive with a decision, remember you asked God for patience. You are being tested to gauge how far you've come or how much farther you have to go, regarding your patience. Beloved, give patience a chance to manifest in your life. Whenever you feel you can't wait on God, just remember that if you wait, He will provide you with the strength to rise and soar. He will give you the stamina to run without getting tired. Even though you may not see Him, He is with you when you undergo pressure, feel distressed, are overwhelmed with trials, and struggle to thrive. He is with you in every unfavorable situation, and every step of the way. He is like oxygen. You can't see it, but you know it's there.

But they that wait upon the Lord shall renew their strength; they shall mount up with wings as eagles; they shall run, and not be weary; and they shall walk, and not faint. Isaiah 40:31^{KJV}

Teach me, Lord, how to wait.

Prayer

Dear Heavenly Father,

I will bless You at all times, and Your praise will continue to be in my mouth. Bless the Lord, O my soul, and all that is within me. Blessed be His Holy name. I adore and love You, unconditionally. Holy Spirit, You are fantastic in my life. You keep me from danger, and You direct my steps. I appreciate You.

Come into my heart Lord Jesus; wash it thoroughly from all sin shame and disgrace. Abba Father, rid me of all unrighteous, folly, and iniquities. In the name of Jesus, cleanse me from every sin that easily besets me. Father God, I surrender my mind, spirit, and body to You.

El-Erekh Apayim, God of patience, thank You for restoring my patience. Abba Father, because of my impatience, I missed numerous opportunities and lost many friends. In the name of Jesus, I ask that you teach me how to exercise patience when I am dealing with others. In Jesus' name. Lord, help me to exercise patience when I am stuck in traffic, standing in line at the cash register, or in the bank, or a restaurant, waiting to be served. In Jesus' name, help me to acknowledge and accept that everyone is different and does things differently.

Abba Father, teach me how to cast my cares upon You, in Jesus' name. Jehovah Rohi, You are my Shepherd; restore my patience, in the name of Jesus. Abba Father, let patience have its perfect work in me that I will be perfect and complete and lacking nothing. Mighty God, in Lamentations 3: 25, You promised that You will be good to those who wait for You and to the soul of those who seek You. In the mighty name of Jesus, teach me how to wait, patiently on You and not run ahead of myself. In the mighty name of Jesus, I reject every spirit of anxiety and worry. Help me not to be anxious for anything but stay calm under Your mighty hands, in Jesus' name. Elohim, may Your peace that passes all understanding keep my heart and mind on Jesus Christ. in Jesus' name. Father, open my spiritual eyes to see trials and trying time as only a test to bring patience and maturity into my life. In Jesus' name.

Thank You, Lord, for being patient with me. Thank You for restoring my patience, thank You for allowing me to, patiently, manage challenging circumstances, in Jesus' mighty name. Blessed be the Lord, forevermore! In Jesus' name, Amen.

And let us not be weary in well doing: for in due season we shall reap, if we faint not. Galatians 6:9^{KJV}

WEEK 29 - RESTORE MY PATIENCE

Notes

Week 30

•••

RESTORE MY WISDOM

He that is slow to anger is better than the mighty; and he that ruleth his spirit than he that taketh a city. (Proverbs 16:32)

Isaac Asimov stated, "The saddest aspect of life right now is that science gathers knowledge faster than society gathers wisdom." *Dr. Charles Stanley* defines wisdom as "Seeing things from God's viewpoint and responding accordingly to scriptural principles." Unfortunately, many of us lack wisdom, both spiritually and physically. For instance, you may have an idea, and without waiting for further instruction from God regarding how and when to approach the idea, you rush to execute it. After facing many obstacles, as a result, you place blame in various directions. However, according to the scripture above, you should consider all aspects of the plan or idea before you start the project. Not every good idea is a God idea, and not every idea that comes to mind should be executed immediately.

Another area in which you may lack wisdom is when confronting an individual who may have caused you pain or hurt. Even though you may be hurting, it shouldn't be your mission to make that individual feel hurt as well. You both deserve to be free of hurt. It would be a great idea to pray and seek God's direction regarding what would be the right time to approach that individual and how to handle the situation beforehand. You know the discomfort and agony you felt as a result of that pain, therefore, as a child of God, you should exhibit care for that individual and not seek revenge.

Beloved, I applaud you for wanting to rectify situations and free your mind and spirit so as to not harbor unforgiveness, resentment, bitterness, anger, or hate. The best approach, when feeling this way, is to exercise humility and have an open heart, ready to forgive and not condemn. By doing so, you invite the opportunity for that individual to clarify their intentions regarding the circumstance. If there are people in your life with whom you have residual issues, continue to seek God's help to let go of the pain you feel; make amends before it is too late.

Here is another way to apply wisdom. If you desire success in your life, identify a mentor or coach to whom you will listen and with whom you will set goals. Connect to those individuals who are doing or have done what you hope to accomplish. Why did God say the children of the world are wiser than the children of light? The children of the world are not afraid to ask for assistance and they pursue their dreams and goals without fear. I encourage you to exercise Godly wisdom in all your decisions. Think before you speak, and plan before you execute. If you listen more and talk less, you will discover extraordinary things.

The evidence of our actions reflects the operation of wisdom.

Dear Heavenly Father,

Your name is worthy of being praised. You are an everlasting Father, and You are the Prince of Peace. Almighty God, how great You are.

Lord, I have sinned against You in my heart and my action. Please forgive me. O, mighty God, I repent for every sin that I have committed. In the name of Jesus, cleanse me from inward sin and carnal weakness.

El Emet, God of truth, Your Word says, "If any of you lack wisdom, let him ask of God, that giveth to all men liberally, and upbraideth not; and it shall be given him." Lord, in the mighty name of Jesus, I present myself to You as an empty vessel needing to be filled with Godly wisdom so that I won't be wise in my own eyes. In the mighty name of Jesus, I use the weapon of wisdom to pull down and destroy the stronghold of folly, in Jesus' mighty name. Father, grant me Your wisdom that is pure, peaceable, gentle, and easily entreated, in the name of Jesus. Lord, endow me with the wisdom that is full of mercy and grace. In the mighty name of Jesus, I receive the wisdom that is without partiality and hypocrisy, in Jesus' name.

In the mighty name of Jesus, I will not lean to my own understanding. Master, I acknowledge You, the Creator of the universe as the only God who gives true wisdom, knowledge, and understanding. El De'ot, God of knowledge, in the name of Jesus, grant me Godly wisdom that I may walk upright and depart from evil. In Jesus' name. Father, help me to walk circumspectly, not as fools but as wise. Holy Spirit, lead and guide my speech; give me a sweet and prudent spirit. May my words be pleasant and laced with wisdom whenever I speak.

Thank You, Abba Father, for restoring my wisdom. Thank You, for allowing my character to exhibit Godly wisdom in everything I do and say. Thank You for the wisdom to know what to say and when to say it. Father God, I promise, from this day forward, wisdom will be my major weapon against folly. Blessed be the Lord, forevermore! In Jesus' name, Amen.

But the wisdom that is from above is first pure, then peaceable, gentle, and easy to be intreated, full of mercy and good fruits, without partiality, and without hypocrisy. James 3:17^{KJV}

Week 30 - Restore My Wisdom

Notes

Week 31

Restore My Compassion

Be kindly affectionate to one another with brotherly love, in honour preferring one another; Romans 12:10^{KJV}

It is a beautiful feeling to demonstrate sympathy and concern for those who are less fortunate, without a hidden agenda. Reaching out with encouragement, sensitivity, and tenderness, for others exemplifies compassion in its pure form. Empathy is a deep inner sensor which sounds whenever someone is in danger and in need. If you find yourself portraying more anger than gentleness, more aggression than meekness, or more intolerance than patience with others, then you have lost the spirit of compassion.

During a conversation with Jesus and His disciples, a lawyer interjected with the intention to tempt Jesus; He asked Jesus how he could inherit eternal life. Jesus answered, *...Thou shalt love the Lord thy God with all thy heart, and with all thy soul, and with all thy strength, and with all thy mind; and thy neighbour as thyself.* Trying to justify himself, again, he asked Jesus, "who is my neighbor?" Thus, Jesus told him a story and asked a follow-up question.

Jesus told the lawyer the following story about a man who journeyed a far distance, and along his journey, he was robbed, beaten, and left for dead. However, a priest and a Levite passed by at separate times and saw the man laying on the side of the road; but both ignored the wounded man's needs and crossed over to the other side of the road. Another man approached, who was rushing to take care of his business, was moved with compassion, so he stopped, cleaned and bandaged the wound, and took the distressed man to an inn, for a safe place to stay. The businessman, not only took him to a place of safety, but paid the innkeeper to take care of the wounded, bleeding stranger. This man is referred to as the good Samaritan. Jesus, then, asked the lawyer, "Who of the three men, would you say is a neighbor to the wounded, bleeding man who was robbed and beaten?" "He who showed mercy," the lawyer answered. Jesus responded, "go and do likewise."

Beloved, have you withheld mercy form anyone who desperately needed you and your assistance? Have you turned a blind eye to those in need? As humans, especially as Christians, we should possess the gifts of compassion and kindness and be ready and willing to lend a helping hand. During Jesus' ministry, He showed compassion to everyone in need without asking for money or notoriety. Remember, He told us in His Word that the least we do unto others, we do it unto Him. Ask God to remove any cold and callous attitude within you and replace it with kindness, mercy, meekness, gentleness, love, and compassion. Lacking sympathy, you may also lack self-control, and you can never determine what or who the enemy may use to pull you out of character, which could cause you to react boisterously and ungodly. Compassion is a mandatory requirement when traveling this pathway of life.

Beloved, allow the Holy Spirit to live out His character through you. God is kind, even to the wicked. Don't be too busy to consider another person's needs. Seek to understand the behavior and character of others so you will know how to treat them. You are the conduit through which God expresses His love and kindness. Your act of compassion can win souls for the kingdom of God. He already told you in His Word how He expects you to treat each other, but ask Him to show you who needs your help and how you can be of assistance to them.

Seeking God's help consistently, through prayer and fasting, will remove negative traits or feelings you experience, as He replaces them with sensitivity, sincerity, and warmth. It is an excellent gesture to treat each other with compassion, especially loved ones at home. Remember, you never know when you may need someone to have mercy and compassion for you. If you have not been genuinely compassionate, it is not too late to start. Plant the seeds, so you can reap a great harvest of mercy.

> *When he saw the crowds, he had compassion on them, because they were harassed and helpless, like sheep without a shepherd.*
>
> Matthew 9:36^{NIV}

Prayer

Dear Heavenly Father,

What a mighty God we serve. Lord, You are the King of Kings and the Lord of Lords, and I worship You. Lord, You are worthy to be praised, magnified, and glorified. I praise Your name.

Compassionate and merciful Father, my heart longs for Your tender touch. Father God, I admit the compassion I have shown to others has been conditional. I show compassion on my own terms, because it makes me feel in control. Hear my cry for help.

El Rachum, God of compassion, had it not been for Your mercies and Your compassion, I would have been consumed. Father God, had it not been for Your great faithfulness, I would have lost my mind. In the mighty name of Jesus, I ask that You restore my compassion and help me to be compassionate to helpless individuals and to those who are spiritually weak.

El Roi, You are the God who sees my every thought and action. In the name of Jesus, I desire to be compassionate. Teach me how to be kind and affectionate, with brotherly love, in Jesus' name. Help me to model the same compassion that You modeled when You were here, on earth, even when no one is watching.

Thank You, Lord, for restoring my compassion. Blessed be the Lord, forevermore! In Jesus' name, Amen.

> *It is of the Lord's mercies that we are not consumed, because his compassions fail not. They are new every morning: great is thy faithfulness. Lamentation 3:22-23^{KJV}*

Notes

Week 32

•••

RESTORE MY VOICE

Cry aloud, spare not, lift up thy voice like a trumpet, and shew my people their transgression, and the house of Jacob their sins.
Isaiah 58:1 ^{KJV}

For too long, you may have been silent, afraid to be heard. Of what are you afraid? Consider what took your voice away and what keeps you silent when you desire to and should speak.

Sexual abuse has disabled the voice of many people because they were threatened with harm if they spoke. Therefore, they assume the blame and guilt, which leaves them feeling unworthy, shameful, and angry.

Lacking the necessary education caused some people to keep silent, believing they would be ridiculed and criticized for not being able to articulate well or speak eloquently. As a result, they are consumed with thoughts of inferiority, intimidation, and insecurity.

Being regularly silenced as a child, teenager, or as an adult, will negatively affect one's confidence and boldness, keeping them silent. Hence, the feelings of intimidation, insignificance, and uselessness take root, and individuals are afraid to speak out against any wrongdoings. In addition, they are even hesitant to give compliments or positive feedback.

Many are scared to take control and speak the truth, fearing what others may say, think, or feel about them. Some individuals believe what they have to say doesn't matter and will not make a difference. However, some may refuse to speak, fearing they will hurt someone's feelings.

Beloved, whatever stole your voice will give it back today. Whoever held your voice hostage will release it today, and if you kept yourself silent out of fear, I rebuke the spirit of fear, in Jesus' name. I command you to take authority over your voice, open your mouth, and be silent no more. If you are worried about hurting someone's feelings when you speak, you are likely doing more harm than good. Ultimately, the truth will set people free. If you allow yourself to speak the truth in love and respect, you may save a life and win a soul for the kingdom of God. *And ye shall know the truth, and the truth shall make you free.* *John 8:32*[KJV].

Some individuals will be comfortable with you remaining stagnant and speechless, but when your voice arises, they will go out of their way to silence you. Do not worry about those who are troubled by your voice, because you are unstoppable and will not be oppressed. Do not be afraid to speak up for yourself.

When Bartimaeus sat blind and helpless on the side of the road, he was rebuked and told to be quiet when he cried out for help from Jesus. Bartimaeus ignored them; and, with boldness, he shouted even louder. With your new-found voice, shout! Regardless of who wants to keep you silenced, and remind them that they did not wake you up or give you life. God needs your voice to speak to the nation, cry out in the wilderness, prophesy to the world, be a witness in the prisons, hospitals, and at home. Your voice must be heard; therefore, renounce and reject the spirit of silence. Open your mouth and praise God, abundantly.

Then they came to Jericho. As Jesus and his disciples, together with a large crowd, were leaving the city, a blind man, Bartimaeus (which means "son of Timaeus"), was sitting by the roadside begging. [47]*When he heard that it was Jesus of Nazareth, he began to shout, "Jesus, Son of David, have mercy on me!"*[48] *Many rebuked him and told him to* be quiet, but he shouted all the more, "Son of David, have mercy on me!"⁴⁹ Jesus stopped and said, "Call him." So they called to the blind man, "Cheer up! On your feet! He's calling you." Mark 10:46-49*NIV*

Fear Not!

Prayer

Dear Heavenly Father,

Thank You for being my everything. You are an amazing God. You are perfect in all of Your ways. In the mighty name of Jesus Christ, God, I seek forgiveness for my sins. Lord, as I present my heart to You today, wash me thoroughly from all my iniquities. Forgive me for allowing the enemy to silence my voice.

O, Mighty God, I ask that You restore my voice. In the powerful name of Jesus, I refuse to be silenced. Father God, the time has come for me to sound the alarm and make the clarion call to Your chosen. In the mighty name of Jesus, deliver me from the spirits of fear, intimidation, dependency, and inadequacy. In the name of Jesus, I will open my mouth and praise You with every breath that I take. In the name of Jesus, I will shout the gospel on the mountain peak. I will share it with everyone that I meet. El Tehilati, God of praise, as of today, I will make a joyful noise unto You. In the name of Jesus, I declare that I will no longer be fearful to open my mouth and use my voice.

In the mighty name of Jesus, I use the weapon of praise to pull down and destroy any stronghold that the enemy is using to silence my voice. Jehovah Eli, Lord God, as I open my mouth to speak, give me your wisdom, knowledge, and understanding. Let me think before I speak and not speak contrary to Your Word, like a fool. Help me to be Holy Spirit-led on what to say and how to say it.

Thank You, Holy Spirit, for empowering me with the boldness to speak without fear. Thank You for restoring my voice. Thank You for hearing and answering my prayer, in Jesus' name. Blessed be the Lord, forevermore! Amen.

> *Cry aloud, spare not, lift up thy voice like a trumpet, and shew my people their transgression, and the house of Jacob their sins.*
>
> *Isaiah 58:1^{KJV}*

Week 32 - Restore My Voice

Notes

Week 33

Restore My Favor

And his master saw that the LORD was with him and that the Lord made all he did to prosper in his hand. And Joseph found grace in his sight, and served him: and he made him overseer over his house, and all that he had he put into his hand. Genesis 39:3-4^{KJV}

On November 16, 2019, I went to the post office to pay for my P.O. box, which was closed for non-payment. When I approached the counter to pay, my card declined. I told the clerk I would return on the 18th. Unfortunately, I could not return until December 11, 2019. I, again, approached the counter to pay, gave her my debit card, and told her I wished to pay for my P.O. box. After confirming my P.O. box number several times, the computer read "payment cannot be accepted after thirty days past due." Nonetheless, the clerk opened my box and returned with a sheet of paper she found inside.

"Miss Gordon, your P.O. box is paid through July 31, 2020. Nothing needs to be done at this time. Just turn in your application. Thank you, signed _____". This was the message written on the note that she found in my box. Talk about favor.

Beloved, when you are obedient to the direction and instruction of God, He will allow people to go beyond their call of duty to extend uncommon favor to you. He will pave the way for you to dine with Kings, give advice to Presidents, and He will endow you with confidence. When your ways please God and your life is satisfactory to Him, He will cause His endorsed favor to open extraordinary doors on your behalf. You will be victorious over the schemes of the enemy, and you will gain preferential treatment and recognition from diplomats. God is getting ready to eject and promote you from your pit into unconditional and extraordinary favor. Favor produces change. Are you prepared to embrace the endorsed favor of God in your life? You will forever testify to the greatness of God.

As of today, I command the unlimited favor of God to be restored upon you so that you will always find favor with men. May the favor of God be restored upon your household, your job, and your business. I pronounce a blessing upon every good thing that you pursue.

It is time to float with me in the ocean of favor.

Prayer

Dear Heavenly Father,

You are the Source from which all blessings flow. You are marvelous, You are superb, and You are wonderful. Hallelujah! Blessed be the matchless name of Jesus. Lord, I repent for everything that I've done, said, or thought that was displeasing to You.

Jehovah Magen, Lord my shield, I come boldly before Your throne of mercy, seeking the restoration of favor in my life, in the name of Jesus. Father, I am saved by Your grace through faith; and because of your unmerited favor, I am alive today. Lord, I remind You of Your promise to bless the righteous, and with favor, You will encircle them with a shield. May Your favor continue to encircle me for the rest of my life. In Jesus' name.

O, mighty God, may Your consuming fire consume anything that is blocking me and preventing favor from locating me. In the name of Jesus, I bind every sabotaging spirit and command them to be stripped from their assignment against my destiny and purpose. Elohim, the living God, restore the kind of favor that no one will overlook me; no one will ignore or, say no to me. Jehovah Naheh, the God who smites, I give You permission to smite every favor stealing demon, in Jesus' name. In Jesus' name, restore the kind of favor that no one can steal or sabotage. In Jesus' name, let me find favor with men as I found with You. In the mighty name of Jesus, grant me the favor that will supernaturally open doors. In the mighty name of Jesus, restore unto me a favor that will make the works of my hands prosper.

Jehovah Sabaoth, Lord of hosts, thank You for restoring unlimited and uncommon favor upon me. May the same favor that rests upon David, Daniel, Joseph, and countless others rest upon me as well. Blessed be the Lord, forevermore! In Jesus' name, Amen.

Surely, Lord, you bless the righteous; you surround them with your favor as with a shield. Psalm 5:12 ^{NIV}

Notes

Week 34

•••

RESTORE MY REVELATION KNOWLEDGE

Fear them not therefore: for there is nothing covered, that shall not be revealed; and hid, that shall not be known. What I tell you in darkness, [that] speak ye in light: and what ye hear in the ear, [that] preach ye upon the housetops. Matthew 10:26-27^{KJV}

Revelation knowledge is God revealing the truth about things you don't actually know. He may disclose information that is currently taking place, something that may have happened in the past, or something to come in the future. Can you imagine having firsthand knowledge of things to come months and years ahead? Or can you imagine having insight about an individual before they approach you for a relationship? I'm sure you would be enthused. It is an indescribable feeling to receive revelation knowledge from God, especially when it enables you to help someone, physically and spiritually.

Ezekiel, the prophet, was captured and was taken away from his home, family, and friends. He was forced into exile by the side of a river. Despite Ezekiel's discomfort and troubles, his spirit was alert and still in tune with God, to the extent that the heavens opened to him, and he saw visions of God. Ezekiel did not allow his immediate condition to interfere with his relationship with God. He was spiritually sharp and precisely described what was revealed to him regarding the future. God was so pleased with Ezekiel, that He revealed Himself to Ezekiel in a powerful way, and Ezekiel was unable to stand on his feet in the presence of God and shekinah glory. If you no longer hear or receive revelation from God, it is time to reposition yourself and check your connection.

How is your relationship with God now compared to when you first met Him? Can God trust you to stay connected to Him when you are going through unfavorable situations? Can He depend on you to make known the visions He reveals to you? Can He still call you a friend? Perhaps you have found yourself in Ezekiel's position, but you allowed the situation to wear you down and snatch you out of the company of God. God is eager to reveal His purpose, His promise, and His power to you, once again. He promises that if you draw closer to Him, He will draw closer to you. Remember, He will not withhold anything from them, who walk in righteousness.

Beloved, God always reveals His plans or the plans of Satan, but you may be too busy to see or hear them. Some individuals receive revelation knowledge through dreams, visions, or written words. For instance, Pharaoh had a dream, but no one could translate or interpret it, except Joseph. For King Belshazzar, a revelation appeared as writing on a wall, and no one could understand or explain it, except Daniel. In these crucial days, the conspiracy of Satan and his cohorts must be unveiled and made known to the body of Christ. God is ready to uncover and reveal the wicked plots, traps, and devices of the enemy now, more than ever before. You need to pay attention and position yourself in the presence of God, continuously, to receive revelation knowledge. In the name of Jesus, I command the restoration of your revelation knowledge.

May your spiritual eyes and ears be opened to the supernatural, and may the heavens be opened unto you.

Prayer

Dear Heavenly Father,

Thank You for Your omnipotence, Your omniscience, and Your omnipresence. Lord, had it not been for You on my side, where would I be? Who would I be? What would my life be without you?

Almighty God, I confess my sins to You today, please forgive me for transgressing against Your law. Forgive me, O God for trespassing against the people who care for me. In the name of Jesus, I sincerely ask that You forgive me for my iniquities.

Father, in the name of Your son, Jesus Christ, I ask that You restore my revelation knowledge. Father God, Your word says that I should call on You, and You will show me great and mighty things which I don't know. In the mighty name of Jesus, I am calling upon You because my soul yearns for Your revelation knowledge. O mighty God, reveal the hidden and secret things to my heart. O God, anything that is hindering me from hearing Your voice or receiving revelation knowledge, I bind it in the mighty name of Jesus and render it powerless.

Almighty God, grant me revelation knowledge about the plans and assignments of the enemy against my life. Teach me, how to strategically combat their schemes, in Jesus' name. I reject the spirit of deafness, blindness, and deception, that are assigned to interfere with my communication with You, O mighty God. In the name of Jesus, I block everything that is trying to block my revelation knowledge.

In the name of Jesus, I command my revelation knowledge to be restored. Father, You said, there will be no secret that will not be revealed and anything hidden will be known and come to the light. Elohim, use me once again to bring revelation knowledge to those who are in the dark. Father, I know that the application of knowledge is power, so, in the name of Jesus, I apply my heart to know, and to search, and to seek out knowledge and wisdom.

Week 34 - Restore My Revelation Knowledge

In the name of Jesus, I ask that You retrain my spirit to understand that which You will reveal, and the knowledge to know how to deal with the revelation. In the name of Jesus, I command my flesh to be in subjection to the Holy Spirit. In the mighty name of Jesus, I command my spiritual ears to be open to hear what the Holy Spirit will reveal unto me.

Thank You, God, for restoring revelation knowledge. Thank You, in advance, for the breakthroughs, victories, power, and uncommon testimonies that will manifest because of the restoration of my revelation knowledge. Blessed be the Lord, forevermore! In Jesus' name, Amen.

*Henceforth I call you not servants; for the servant knoweth not what his lord doeth: but I have called you **FRIENDS**; for all things that I have heard of my Father I have made known unto you. John 15:15 KJV*

DAILY RESTORATIONAL

Notes

Week 35

•••

RESTORE MY FINANCES

He becometh poor that dealeth with a slack hand: but the hand of the diligent maketh rich. Proverbs 10:4 ^{KJV}

Many of us face financial strife, for one reason or another. Sometimes, regardless of your efforts, you are still unable to make ends meet. Many reasons can cause this financial dilemma. For example, overspending, lack of planning, lack of budgeting, living outside of your means, and failure to be a good steward of your money. Financial lack can also be the effect of spiritual wickedness in high places which forces you to spend frivolously until your money is depleted. Further, refusing to tithe can also be one of the biggest and most detrimental reasons why your finances are under attack.

It is possible that your finances are being attacked by the spirit of mammon, principalities, powers, or rulers of darkness. Their objective is for you to remain poverty-stricken, always begging, borrowing, never having enough, and unable to get out of debt. Therefore, you are forced to live beneath your potential, unless you compromise the Word of God to worship and serve them. Below, Jesus clearly expresses that we cannot serve two masters at the same time.

No servant can serve two masters: for either he will hate the one, and love the other; or else he will hold to the one, and despise the other. **Ye cannot serve God and mammon.** Luke 16: 13$^{KJV.}$

To explain, mammon is associated with money but does not mean money, as many believe. Mammon is the spirit that governs or controls money-a spirit which desires to be served and worshipped. It emphasizes that when you have riches, you don't need God. For those who reject mammon's offer and choose God instead, mammon does everything in its power to sabotage and withhold their finances. Mammon promises happiness, joy, peace, stability, and self-worth. Mammon over-promises and under-delivers. Falling for the promises of mammon will cost you, dearly. Unlike mammon, you don't have to do anything extraordinary for God to supply all your needs, whether you serve Him or not. *That ye may be the children of your Father which is in heaven:* **for he maketh his sun to rise on the evil and on the good, and sendeth rain on the just and on the unjust.** *Matthew 5:45^{KJV}*.

The spirit of mammon encourages individuals to disobey God and His Word, with regards to tithing. It presents as a voice in your ear, creating excuses for why tithing is not relevant, which suggests that one doesn't have to tithe anymore. Beloved, it is in your best interest to begin tithing, if you haven't started, yet. God does not revoke His promises. Matthew 24:35 says *Heaven and earth shall pass away, but my words shall not pass away.* Therefore, if a lack of tithing is the cause of the rift in your finances, you know what you need to do.

God asks for only ten cents out of your dollar. For you committing to give that ten cents, He guarantees you an overflow of blessings, a house of abundance, His protection over your finances, honor, among other assurances. What more could you ask for? His promises are sure. Beloved, if your financial situation is not caused by carelessness or lack of tithing, you must counter-attack and cancel the assignment against your finances, which is orchestrated by mammon, principalities, powers, and rulers of darkness. Command the restoration of your finances, in Jesus' name. Pray the promises of God over yourself, daily.

I decree and declare there will be no more financial drought in your life. It is not the will of God for you to lack daily necessities when He promises to supply your needs and desires. He wants you to prosper, so you must become radical and put a command on your money.

Below are additional scriptures which share God's promises for you and your money:

¹²Both riches and honour come of thee, and thou reignest over all; and in thine hand is power and might; and in thine hand it is to make great, and to give strength unto all. 1 Chronicles 29:12^(KJV)

⁵Now therefore thus saith the Lord of hosts; Consider your ways. ⁶Ye have sown much, and bring in little; ye eat, but ye have not enough; ye drink, but ye are not filled with drink; ye clothe you, but there is none warm; and he that earneth wages earneth wages to put it into a bag with holes. Haggai 1:5-6^(KJV)

¹⁰ So shall thy barns be filled with plenty, and thy presses shall burst out with new wine. Proverbs 3:10^(KJV)

¹¹And I will rebuke the devourer for your sakes, and he shall not destroy the fruits of your ground; neither shall your vine cast her fruit before the time in the field, saith the Lord of hosts. Malachi 3:11^(KJV)

³⁸ Give, and it shall be given unto you; good measure, pressed down, and shaken together, and running over, shall men give into your bosom. For with the same measure that ye mete withal it shall be measured to you again. Luke 6:38^(KJV)

⁵Trust in the Lord with all thine heart; and lean not unto thine own understanding. ⁶In all thy ways acknowledge him, and he shall direct thy paths. ⁷Be not wise in thine own eyes: fear the Lord, and depart from evil. ⁸It shall be health to thy navel, and marrow to thy bones. ⁹Honour the Lord with thy substance, and with the firstfruits of all thine increase: ¹⁰So shall thy barns be filled with plenty, and thy presses shall burst out with new wine. Proverbs 3:5-10^(KJV)

⁶But this I say, He which soweth sparingly shall reap also sparingly; and he which soweth bountifully shall reap also bountifully. ⁷Every man according as he purposeth in his heart, so let him give; not grudgingly, or of necessity: for God loveth a cheerful giver. ⁸And God is able to make all grace abound toward you; that ye, always having all sufficiency in *all things, may abound to every good work: 2 Corinthians 9:6-8^{KJV}*

^{10}*Bring ye all the tithes into the storehouse, that there may be meat in mine house, and prove me now herewith, saith the Lord of hosts, if I will not open you the windows of heaven, and pour you out a blessing, that there shall not be room enough to receive it. Malachi 3:10^{KJV}*

Money answers all things.

Prayer

Dear Heavenly Father,

Thank You for reigning in victory. I worship and adore You. I glorify Your name. Thank You for preserving me.

Abba Father, I confess, I have been a terrible manager over the finances that You entrusted in my care. O mighty God, please forgive me for squandering my finances. Forgive me for not being a good steward over my finances. Father God, please forgive me for robbing you in tithe and offering. Forgive me for being a spendthrift. Forgive me, O, God, for sowing sparingly and grudgingly and deliver me from the spirit of stinginess. El Yeshuati, God of my salvation, please wash me thoroughly from all unrighteousness and set me free, in the name of Jesus. Father, because of my selfishness towards You, I realize that I have been earning wages but putting it into a bag with holes, according to Haggai 1:6.

In the mighty name of Jesus, I use the weapon of abundance to pull down and destroy the stronghold of lack and poverty. I decree and declare that, as of today, I will not put my money in any more bags with holes. In the name of Jesus, I will not be the borrower, but be a lender. I will not be beneath, but above. I will not be a curse, but a blessing, in the mighty name of Jesus. Through the power in the blood of Jesus Christ, I will no longer live in lack or poverty, but in abundance and overflow. In the mighty name of Jesus, I stand on Your Word, believing that money answers all things, and You wish for me to prosper even as my soul prospers.

Jehovah Naheh, smite and paralyze the spirit of mammon that is sabotaging my finances, in the mighty name of Jesus. I bind every stealing spirit that is assigned to steal my finances, in Jesus' name. I bind and render powerless, every evil work of the devil, against my finances and prosperity, in Jesus' name.

Thank You for the restoration of my finances. Thank You for supernaturally releasing money and assets, in my life now, in Jesus' name. Elyon, the most high God, thank You for Your guidance into being a better steward over my business and finances. Thank You for teaching me how to sow into fertile soil. Lord, Thank You for teaching me how to give bountifully and cheerfully, in Jesus name. Father God, thank You for teaching me how to honor You with my money, so my house will be filled with food at all times. Thank You for releasing favor and prosperity upon me, in the mighty name of Jesus. Blessed be the Lord, forevermore! In Jesus' name, Amen.

The rich ruleth over the poor and the borrower is servant to the lender. Proverbs 22:7 KJV

Notes

Week 36

•••

Restore My Possessions

After Job had prayed for his friends, the Lord restored his fortunes and gave him twice as much as he had before. Job 42:10^{NIV}

Many individuals suffer from mental health issues after the loss of a spouse or family member. Some become depressed because they lost their job, business, or investments, while many suffer, given the loss of their houses, cars, money, and other material things. What have you lost? Has anything been stolen from you? Have you ever experienced a repossession of your vehicle or your furniture or the foreclosure of your home? If so, today is the day you will rise with fire in your mouth to destroy the devourer and anything which has deprived you of your possessions. Not only do you need these things to be restored, but it is time to claim your promised possessions.

The Israelites, after being robbed of their birthright, were captured and taken to Egypt, where they were severely abused. They were enslaved, beaten, used, tortured, and patronized at the hand of Pharaoh and his followers. Some were even killed. When God saw the ill-treatment of His people, He intervened and used His power to free them by sending numerous plagues, tribulations, and even death upon Pharaoh and his armies. For his people, God handpicked a prime piece of land in Canaan, filled to its capacity with fruit trees, milk, and honey-everything the people needed to survive and thrive. However, before they occupied the land, Moses sent twelve men as spies to search out the land. After 40 days, the spies returned to Moses and the congregation, and ten of them reported that "the land is flowing with milk and honey, and it is fruitful, but:

> The people who dwell in the land are very strong;
>
> The cities are surrounded by huge walls;
>
> We saw the children of Anak there;
>
> The Amalekites dwell in the land to the south;
>
> The Hittites, Jebusites, and the Amorites dwell in the mountain;
>
> The Canaanites dwell by the sea and by the coast;
>
> We are not able to possess the land with those giants;
>
> We are like grasshoppers in their eyes;
>
> These people are stronger than us;
>
> The land eats up the inhabitants."

After they listed the reasons why they couldn't happily possess their promised land, Caleb, one of the twelve spies, got the attention of Moses and the others and said, *30Let us go up at once, and possess it; for we are well able to overcome it. The ten doubters responded, 31But the men that went up with him said, We be not able to go up against the people; for they are stronger than we. The land, through which we have gone to search it, is a land that eateth up the inhabitants thereof; and all the people that we saw in it are men of a great stature. Numbers 13:30-32*[KJV]

Upon hearing such a negative report, the children of Israel wept all night and murmured their discontentment against Moses, Aaron, and God. They grumbled amongst themselves and said they wished they had died in the land of Egypt or died in the wilderness. Instead, they felt God brought them to the land so they could be killed by the sword, and their families would suffer. They questioned whether it would have been better to be left in Egypt. "Forget about Moses, let us appoint a new leader who will lead us back to Egypt," they said. When Moses and Aaron heard the ungratefulness, they collapsed

Week 36 - Restore My Possessions

out of sorrow and disbelief, while Joshua and Caleb, the positive two of the twelve spies, tore their clothes as a sign of grief. Joshua and Caleb spoke to the congregation of the sons of Israel, and said, ... *The land, which we passed through to search it, is an exceedingly good land. ⁸If the Lord delight in us, then he will bring us into this land, and give it to us; a land which floweth with milk and honey. ⁹Only rebel not ye against the Lord; neither fear ye the people of the land; for they are bread for us: their defence is departed from them, and the Lord is with us: fear them not.. ¹⁰But all the congregation bade stone them with stones. And the glory of the Lord appeared in the tabernacle of the congregation before all the children of Israel. Numbers 14:7-10ᴷᴶⱽ*

Beloved, do you often focus on the negative more than the positive? What excuses do you use to talk yourself out of your promised possessions? Who or what are you allowing to plant seeds of doubt in your mind? What are the reasons why you haven't received God's best for your life? Why do you say you love God but refuse to trust Him to do what is best for you? It is time to possess your position, but like most things, there are requirements.

Your heavenly Father wants you to inherit His best. He wants you to be delivered from your enemies and be freed from oppression, as you experience unlimited peace. The giants will always be present, but as was David, you are anointed and equipped with weapons to slay giants. However, victory may require repentance and a turning away from your iniquities, transgressions, and sin. Renew your mindset and take authority over your life so you may possess your promised possessions. No longer be afraid. *Behold, I give unto you power to tread on serpents and scorpions, and overall the power of the enemy: and nothing shall by any means hurt you. Luke 10:19ᴷᴶⱽ*

To defeat and conquer, you must identify your giants, whether it is broken marriage, financial troubles, or self-sabotage, and destroy their influence and power over your life. God is bigger than any giant you can or cannot see. Just trust His power within you, you are a giant slayer.

God promises that He will subdue your enemies. He promised that your enemies would come into your life one way, but they will flee from you several ways. Remember, when the enemy comes in like a flood, The Spirit of the Lord will lift up a standard against them, and God will give His angels charge over you, for protection.

Don't listen to those who don't see your vision for freedom, change, and independence. Whether it's furthering your education or starting a business, all it takes is a made-up mind and consistency. The few naysayers along your journey and people who lack vision, trust, and belief, can cause you to lose the freedom and wealth you already own. Do not let your dreams be compromised because of the fears and negative spirits of others.

10 necessary keys to gain your promised possessions:

- A positive spirit
- A relentless faith and trust in God
- An unshakeable belief
- Boldness/ Courage
- Tenacity
- Complete obedience
- Surround yourself with like-minded people
- Grow tired of watching others succeed; pursue your dreams.
- Renounce fear
- Have a grateful heart and a positive mindset

Surely all the men who have seen My glory and My [miraculous] signs which I performed in Egypt and in the wilderness, yet have put Me to the test these ten times and have not listened to not one of those who saw my glory and the signs I performed in Egypt and in the wilderness but who disobeyed me and tested me ten times— ²³*not one of them will ever see the land I promised on oath to their ancestors. No one who has treated me with contempt will ever see it. ²⁴But because my servant Caleb has a different spirit and follows me wholeheartedly, I will bring him into the land he went to, and his descendants will inherit it. Numbers 14:22-24*^{NIV}

Stop running. Tackle your giants, and overtake them.

Prayer

Dear Heavenly Father,

Father, I am glad You are the God who I can call any time and don't have to make an appointment to speak with or be transferred to a voicemail or Your secretary. Holy Spirit, You have been so faithful, merciful, and kind. Abba Father, I will be forever grateful for all You have done for me, to me, through me, and with me. Words cannot explain.

Dear God, I repent of all my sins-known and unknown. Create in me a clean heart, O God, and renew the right spirit within me. God of restoration, I humble myself before You, seeking Your forgiveness for every sin I've committed. Wash me thoroughly from my iniquities, deliver me from my shortcomings, and set me free from my idiosyncrasies, which open the door for the enemy to inflict pain into my life.

Elyashiv, the God who restores, I ask that You restore my possessions. For too long, the works of my hands seem to be futile and have come to naught. Lord, everything I do or own is being tampered with or sabotaged, so I come boldly before Your throne of mercy to remind You of Your promises and Your desire for my life. In the name of Jesus, Your only begotten Son, I come asking You to intervene in this situation. Father, in 3John 1:2 You said, "Beloved, I wish above all things that thou mayest prosper and be in health, even as thy soul prospereth." According to Deuteronomy 28: 1-14, You said, if I listen diligently to Your voice and obey Your command, You will set me on high, above all nations of the earth and my blessings will overtake me. Lord, You promised that wherever I go I will be blessed. My children will be blessed, and You will command blessings upon me in my storehouses and all the works of my hands. You promised to make me the head and not the tail, the lender and not the borrower, above only and not beneath.

In the mighty name of Jesus Christ, I stand on these promises and rest under the shadow of Your mighty hands, believing that whatever I bind on earth, You will bind in heaven and whatever I loose on earth, You will loose it in heaven. In the mighty name of Jesus, I bind every locust, caterpillar, cankerworm, and devourer. May Your consuming fire consume them right now. Through the power in the blood of Jesus, I release my angels to confiscate the weapons of my enemies, repossess my belongings, and restore them unto me, in Jesus' name. Jehovah Naheh, You are the Lord who smites, I ask Your permission to release warrior angels to help me fight and smite the giants who captured my possessions.

Satan, the blood of Jesus Christ is against you and your agents. I command you to release all you have stolen and held captive from me, right now, in the name of Jesus. Father God, I hide behind the shield of faith, knowing that You will give Your angels charge over me. I hide behind the shield of faith, believing that Your angels will hold me up in their hands and protect me from the traps planted by the enemy. Jehovah Jireh, Your Word said to remind You of Your promises. Therefore I am reminding You of Deuteronomy 6:11 which declares that You promise houses I did not build- houses filled to capacity with food I did not buy- wells I did not dig, and vineyards I did not plant.

Jehovah-Gibbor, the Lord mighty in battle; thank You for the power to trample upon lions, adder, dragons, and young lions and anything else that interfered with my possessions. Thank You for delivering me and setting me in a high place, away from my enemies who seek my demise. Thank You, Lord, for allowing me to see my enemies when they came in one way and fled seven ways. Thank You for smiting them before my face, when they rise up against me without a cause. Thank You for Your promise to open Your good treasure in heaven and rain down more blessings in my position. Thank You for establishing me so that all people can see that I am called by the name of Jesus Christ. O, Covenant keeping God, thank You for restoring my possessions. Blessed be the Lord, forevermore! In Jesus' name, Amen.

Come now, and let us reason together, saith the LORD: though your sins be as scarlet, they shall be as white as snow; though they be red like crimson, they shall be as wool. If ye be willing and obedient, ye shall eat the good of the land. But if ye refuse and rebel, ye shall be devoured with the sword: for the mouth of the LORD hath spoken it. Isaiah 1:18-20[KJV]

Notes

Week 37

•••

Restore My Community

For we wrestle not against flesh and blood, but against principalities, against powers, against the rulers of the darkness of this world, against spiritual wickedness in high places. Ephesians 6:12^{KJV}

Many factors can contribute to the desolation of a community. Being economically challenged is a major factor for most. Others include ongoing violence and the lack of psychological, physiological, educational, and spiritual guidance and support. Any community which experiences unusually negative activities may be under a demonic curse. Some agents of Satan are assigned to cast spells and curses on communities, families, individuals, churches, schools, etc.

A young man named John Ramirez shared his testimony regarding how, as a Satan high priest, one of his primary assignments was to cast spells and curses on different regions. He stated that one night he astral projected (left his body) and entered a particular neighborhood to cast a spell and place a curse on the community. However, upon arrival, four women stood on the side of the street, holding hands and were praying for the community for hours. As a result, he was unable to execute his evil mission. He further stated that the only neighborhoods or communities in which he was unsuccessful in his evil endeavors were communities where people were praying. (see his testimony in its entirety on YouTube)

When communities are under demonic siege, there is little to no fear of God in that community. Those communities may experience more murder, rape, poverty, insanity, illiteracy, and unexplained death, at an alarming rate. In contrast, other communities may willfully engage in witchcraft, obeah, black magic, voodoo, or cultic activities. Yes, it is possible those communities were cursed. When a community is overwhelmed with the aforementioned afflictions, some of the residents may become perturbed, fearless, lawless, or hopeless. Sadly, if a place is under siege by demonic forces, no organization, government, multi-billionaire, president, prime minister, Queen, or earthly King can restore it.

As a sincere, born-again child of God, you have the power to bring order and restoration to that community using prayer, praise, worship, fasting, and the Word of God along with the blood of Jesus. However, you must first identify the areas of struggle in that community and bind those issues, according to the Word of God. *Or else how can one enter into a strong man's house, and spoil his goods, except he first bind the strong man? and then he will spoil his house. Matthew 12:9^{KJV}* When the strong man is paralyzed, you will be better able to defeat the territorial spirits which operate under the strong man and rule that territory and the minds of the people. You have the necessary weapon to win the war against the spiritual battle plaguing your community.

God has given you dominion over your territory; don't be intimidated.

Dear Heavenly Father,

You are so loving and faithful to me. How great and majestic is Your name. Holy Spirit, I honor and adore You.

Abba Father, I come, boldly before You, seeking Your forgiveness for all my sins. Lord, I repent for participating in sinful acts that prevented me from getting closer to You. Father God, I repent of the sin that prevented my prayers from being answered. Almighty God, please forgive me for anything that I have done to displease You.

Week 37 - Restore My Community

In the mighty name of Jesus, I remit the sin of my community to You. Forgive us, O, God for sins committed, known and unknown. Elohim, on behalf of my community, I repent of all wickedness, iniquities, trespasses, and transgression. In the mighty name of Jesus, I break and destroy every covenant made with Satan, against my community.

In the mighty name of Jesus, I ask that You restore my community. Matthew 3:27 reminds me that, "No man can enter into a strong man's house, and spoil his goods, except he will first bind the strong man, and then he will spoil his house." In the name of Jesus Christ, the only begotten son of God, I bind up the strong man of my community and I render his works powerless, null, and void. In the name of Jesus Christ, I bind up every assignment plotted against my community. I bind strong man of smoking, drinking, gambling, pornography, and poverty, that held the occupants of the community in bondage. In Jesus' name.

Through the power in the blood of Jesus Christ, I bind the strong man that is behind all illness, infirmity, and affliction. In the name of Jesus, I bind up all religious spirit that has come to brainwash the people of the community and turn their mind from Christ. Jehovah Naheh, I bind and rendered powerless the spirit of untimely death in my community, in Jesus' name. I bind and destroy every demonic or idol worship in this community, in Jesus' name. Jehovah, Naheh, the God who smites, please release Uriel and Michael, Your archangels, to smite and destroy the spirits of murder, rape, incest, lack, death, witchcraft, necromancy, sorcery, psychic reading, and any other evil spirits and their assignments against my community.

Lord, I know the weapon of our warfare is not carnal but mighty through You to the pulling down of all strongholds. O, mighty God, I use the weapon of love to pull down the stronghold of hate and murder in my community, in Jesus mighty name. I use the weapon of hope to pull down the stronghold of despair, in Jesus' name. I use the weapon of faith and boldness, to pull down the stronghold of fear, In the mighty name of Jesus. I use the weapon of victory, to pull down the stronghold of defeat, the weapon of deliverance, to pull down the stronghold of oppression and depression, in Jesus' mighty name.

In the powerful name of Jesus, I use the weapon of abundance to destroy the stronghold of poverty and lack- the weapon of wisdom to pull down the stronghold of folly- the weapon of health to destroy all illness, infirmity, and affliction, in Jesus' mighty name. Adonai, in the name of Jesus, I use the weapon of success to annihilate the stronghold of failure. Jehovah Mephalti, my deliver, in the name of Jesus, I use the weapon of prayer to bind and destroy all evil assignment against my community and its residents. El Tehilati, God of praise, I use the weapon of praise and worship to confuse and frustrate every evil counsel taken against my community and it's residents, in Jesus' name. Abba Father, in the mighty name of Jesus, I command our weapons of fasting and prayer to frustrate the wicked, along with their conspiracy. In the name of Jesus, I release the consuming fire of God to uproot and destroy all curses, spells, rituals, incantations, and hexes.

Jehovah Naheh, I reclaim this community from the workers of iniquity. May your consuming fire destroy principalities, powers, rulers of darkness, and spiritual wickedness in high places that are oppressing and mutilating the people of this community, in the name of Jesus. In the name of Jesus, I command you, tormenting spirits, not to re-enter my community or its residents again, in Jesus' name. Lord, everything that was broken and destroyed, I cast them out into outer darkness and dry places, in Jesus' name. I cover the entire community and its residents with the blood of Jesus Christ.

Jehovah Shalom, God of peace, thank You for restoring tranquility and peace in my community. Thank You for Your protection over my community, in the mighty name of Jesus. I release the love of God in the community and its residents, in Jesus' mighty name. With the power vested in me, I speak freedom and deliverance over the minds, spirits, health, and finances of all residents in this community, in Jesus' name. Blessed be the Lord, forevermore! In Jesus' name, Amen.

Lest Satan should get an advantage of us: for we are not ignorant of his devices. 2 Corinthians 2:11^{KJV}

Daily Restorational

Notes

_____ *Week 38*

•••

RESTORE THE CHURCH

For yourselves know perfectly that the day of the Lord so cometh as a thief in the night. Therefore let us not sleep, as do others; but let us watch and be sober..1 Thessalonians 5:2 & 6^{KJV}

*C*hurch is often considered a building. However, we are the church, and we assemble in a building to encourage, uplift, and strengthen each other as "iron sharpens iron". Therefore, as the church, we can celebrate Jesus Christ wherever we are and restore a divine relationship with Him. *Husbands, love your wives, just as Christ loved the church and gave himself up for her ^{26}to make her holy, cleansing her by the washing with water through the word, ^{27}and to present her to himself as a radiant church, without stain or wrinkle or any other blemish, but holy and blameless. Ephesians 5:25-27^{NIV}*

As the body of Christ, we are about to undergo grave persecution and oppression. The temporary shutdown of churches, given the pandemic, is a glimpse of what's to come. During tough times like these, the church needs to be awakened and restored. COVID-19 has exposed the strength, readiness, trust, faith, and weaknesses of many saints of God. Jeremiah 12: 25 asked, *if thou hast run with the footmen, and they have wearied thee, then how canst thou contend with horses? and if in the land of peace, wherein thou trustedst, they wearied thee, then how wilt thou do in the swelling of Jordan?* In other words, if you cannot endure the tough times of today, how will you withstand the treacherous times of tomorrow?

Though worship services using social media is helpful, it does not compare to assembling with one another, touching and agreeing, for there is power in agreement. Psalm 122:1[KJV] says, *I was glad when they said unto me, Let us go into the house of the Lord.* Psalm 133:1[KJV] says *Behold, how good and how pleasant it is for brethren to dwell together in unity!* Hebrews 10:25[KJV] reminded us, *Not forsaking the assembling of ourselves together, as the manner of some is; but exhorting one another: and so much the more, as ye see the day approaching.* Saints, arise. The end of the world as we know it is fast approaching, whether you want to believe it or not. I urge you to read Matthew 24. Nevertheless, God, with His infinite mercy, counts on our restoration, as we rise again to sound the alarm.

Church, it is time to rebuild the altars for the true and living God. Do not be ignorant of the devil's device, for Satan always has a plan to strip God's people of their authority and power. It is time to restore the message of the gospel of the kingdom of God without watering it down. It is that gospel which will pluck us out of the vice grip of the enemy and thrust us into the arms of Jesus Christ. *And this gospel of the kingdom shall be preached in all the world for a witness unto all nations; and then shall the end come. Matthew 24:14.* Now is the time to restore the outreach ministries and begin harvesting souls for God. Most importantly, let us pray for the restoration of the supernatural power to be activated in the church once again. With the supernatural power activated, it will pave the way for the fivefold ministries and the spiritual gifts to operate.

Church, God eagerly awaits our return to sacrificing. He calls for the sacrifice of praise, prayer, worship, thanksgiving, and good deeds. *By him therefore let us offer the sacrifice of praise to God continually, that is, the fruit of our lips giving thanks to his name. [16]But to do good and to communicate forget not: for with such sacrifices God is well pleased. Hebrews 13:15-16[KJV].* As mentioned in Romans 12:1 NIV, He is patiently waiting for us to present our bodies as living sacrifices, holy and pleasing to God. Beloved, out of our submission and obedience to Him, the church will be restored to take hold of our spiritual inheritance.

May the supernatural power of God endow you, again.

Prayer

Dear Heavenly Father,

I cry out to You today on behalf of the church. The coming together as a body of Christ is in grave danger.

Father, forgive us for falling asleep and falling into a spiritual coma. Jehovah Tsidkenu, You are the Lord of righteousness. In the name of Jesus, cleanse us from all our ungodly ways, and deliver us from our lackadaisical attitudes. Abba, Father, as we rebuild the walls and Your altar, I ask that You would restore unto the church Your supernatural power. Father, restore unto Your church the apostle, teacher, pastor, evangelist, and prophet (The fivefold ministry). I petition to You on behalf of the outreach ministries; El Yashiv, restore our passion for evangelism and mission ministries, in Jesus' name.

Jehovah Hashe'ah, You are the Lord who saves, I pray for the restoration of families, in Jesus' name. In the mighty name of Jesus, I ask that You heal and restore the relationships between spouses and children; and bring them back together, again. God, we need You now more than ever. Give us the strength to overcome the attacks of the enemy. In the mighty name of Jesus, I ask that you strengthen us so we won't crumble under pressure. All sufficient God, we believe and stand firm on Your Word that You will be with us until the end of time. I know that You will never leave nor forsake us.

In the mighty name of Jesus, I use the weapon of prayer, praise, worship, and fasting to pull down and destroy the stronghold of evil counsel, demonic sabotage, frustration, and confusion that rise up against Your church. Lord, El Gibbor, hear our cry from Your sanctuary. We anticipate a speedy restoration of the church-a church without spot or wrinkle, in Jesus' name. Abba Father, restore a church that will not be lukewarm. Restore a church that will not compromise Your Word but will be bold, in the face of atrocity. O mighty God, restore the kind of church that will cramp, paralyze, and destroy the works of demons and devils, in Jesus' name.

Glory to God. Master, I say thank You for not dealing with us with Your sore displeasure. Thank You, Jehovah Nissi, for Your promise to protect. Thank You, Jehovah Ganan, for being our defense. Thank You, Jehovah Neheh, for smiting those who rise up against this community. Thank You, Jehovah Rophe for healing the community. Omnipotent God, thank You for the restoration of Your church. Blessed be the Lord, forevermore! In Jesus' name, Amen.

This know also, that in the last days perilous times shall come. ²For men shall be lovers of their own selves, covetous, boasters, proud, blasphemers, disobedient to parents, unthankful, unholy, ³Without natural affection, trucebreakers, false accusers, incontinent, fierce, despisers of those that are good, ⁴Traitors, heady, highminded, lovers of pleasures more than lovers of God; ⁵ Having a form of godliness, but denying the power thereof: from such turn away.

2 Timothy 3:1-5^{KJV}

Notes

Week 39

•••

Restore My Hearing

Therefore the heart of the king of Syria was sore troubled for this thing; and he called his servants, and said unto them, Will ye not shew me which of us is for the king of Israel? And one of his servants said, None, my lord, O king: but Elisha, the prophet that is in Israel, telleth the king of Israel the words that thou speakest in thy bedchamber. 2 Kings 6:11-12^{KJV}

During an advertisement promoting hearing-aids, it was said that over 40% of individuals over the age of 50 suffer from hearing loss. The most common reasons for hearing loss are aging and a prolonged period of background noise, but not limited to. Regularly, patients visit their doctor with what they presume to be a hearing problem, or they feel unsteady when standing or walking. After a thorough examination of the ear, one patient was told, "you don't have hearing loss; the inner ear is blocked by wax, and your sinuses are infected, which affects your hearing. If we can remove the wax and sinusitis, your hearing will be excellent." The patient with the balancing problem thought the issue was dizziness or skeletal-related, however, they suffered from hearing loss. Compromised hearing can, ultimately, affect balance.

Many individuals wonder if God still speaks to us. Some may say, "I believe He speaks, but I cannot hear Him", while others are adamant that He no longer speaks. God still speaks to His people, today. Therefore, you must reflect on the following questions: Do you have an intimate relationship with God? Have you surrendered your life to Him? Has your spirit yielded to Him? Consider these testimonies:

Week 39 - Restore My Hearing

In the year 2011, I was searching for an apartment to live. When I visited the first one, I heard the Lord say "no servant of mine will live here". Shortly after, I saw a young man nearby, and I asked him if he knew of any houses or apartments for rent. He said he did but emphasized, from his personal experience, that I wouldn't want to live there. He was referring to the same building God advised me against.

I continued my search and visited a complex I was referred to by a young lady. I heard God say "I don't want you to live here", but I ignored the voice and continued with the process. When completing the rental application, the voice was re-emphasized about not living there. I ignored the voice again and finished the necessary paperwork. While trying to process my paperwork, the office manager encountered countless hurdles, as my verification could not be completed. At that point, I had to return to work, and upon arrival, a voice told me "put your clothes in storage." The next day, I found a storage unit and asked the clerk for any positive apartment referrals. She didn't know of any, but she advised me against living in the same apartment complex with which I recently experienced glitches in the processing and verification of my application.

Who says God no longer speaks? *"I will instruct thee and teach thee in the way which thou shalt go: I will guide thee with mine eye. 9 Be ye not as the horse, or as the mule, which have no understanding: whose mouth must be held in with bit and bridle, lest they come near unto thee." Psalm 32:8-9^{KJV}*

Additionally, in March of 2019, I was planning my 50th birthday gala, which was scheduled for April of 2020. I wanted it to be extravagant. I filled my online cart with unique accessories and was going to complete my purchase, when I heard a voice say, "wait". During that year, I tried numerous times to purchase the items, and I kept hearing the same voice say "wait." When March of 2020 arrived, less than four weeks away from my gala, I finally decided to buy the items from the online cart, given the time constraints. When I was about to complete the purchase, I heard, "don't buy them". Thereafter, I logged off without buying the items, figuring I would purchase them the following week. The next week, the arrival of COVID-19 was announced, hence, a mandatory cancellation of the gala due to the prohibiting of large gatherings. Who says God no longer speaks?

Beloved, it is crucial to be able to hear and differentiate the voice of God. He cares about every detail of your life, no matter how insignificant they may seem to you. He always speaks, whether through dreams, visions, prophecy, His Word, or by a whisper within your spirit. If you have ever said, "my mind told me to…", that could be the voice of God speaking to you, but your connection may be spiritually corroded. If you think God is not speaking to you, check the connection between you and God. Check to see what could be interfering with your frequency and blocking the reception in your spiritual ears. What background noise are you allowing to override the voice of God? What is distracting you? Perhaps your environment is so noisy and confusing that you cannot tell whose voice you are hearing. As a result, you marry the wrong person, live in the wrong neighborhood, involve yourself with the wrong business, or choose the wrong career.

Hearing God demands quietness, alone time, and steadfastness. To restore your spiritual hearing, you must get out of the crowd, turn down the volume of the background noise, step away from some people and some things. Seek to spend time meditating on His Word with humility. By doing so, you will learn which method of communication He wants to use to speak with you. *The unfolding of your words gives light; it gives understanding to the simple. Psalm 119:130*. It is prudent that you walk in obedience with what you hear God say, and follow His instructions; it may save your life. It is not enough to be a hearer of the Word only, but be a doer as well. Faith without works is dead. Get closer to God and make sure your hearing is in line with His voice.

Hearing and obeying the voice of the Holy Spirit will protect your soul and save your life.

Week 39 - Restore My Hearing

Prayer

Dear Heavenly Father,

I celebrate and reverence Your name. Thank You for Your guidance and counsel. Your name is worthy to be praised. You are Alpha, and Omega. I worship You O Sovereign God.

O Lord, my redeemer, I come boldly before Your throne of grace, seeking Your forgiveness as I repent for the sins I committed. Search my heart O God, remove all wicked thoughts found within me. Father God, empty me of all impurities, inward sin, and carnal weakness, in Jesus' name.

Jehovah Bara, Lord my Creator, I ask that You restore my spiritual hearing, in Jesus' mighty name. Father, I have allowed my hearing to be contaminated by the noise of the world. O, Father God, I ask that You remove every spiritual blockage, toxin, and corrosion from my spiritual ears, in Jesus' name. In the mighty name of Jesus, I command my spiritual hearing to be blocked against the toxin from social media, corrupt communication, and bad influence from associates. Restore, O God.

In the mighty name of Jesus, I use the weapon of awareness to pull down the stronghold of ignorance, deafness, and confusion. I release the spirit of comprehension, knowledge, and consciousness upon me, right now. I use the weapon of awareness to destroy every evil counsel, demonic sabotage, and conspiracy assigned against my spiritual and physical ears. Lord, with great expectation, I look forward to the restoration of my hearing. Abba Father, I desire to hear and identify Your voice clearly. In the mighty name of Jesus, I also desire to hear the plans and plots of the enemy, against me.

Lord, Your Word says that Your sheep know Your voice, and a stranger they will not follow. Teach me how to identify Your voice, with clarity. Teach me how to be alert to Your whispers. Holy Spirit,

I surrender my spiritual ears to You. Thank You, El Elyon, for restoring my hearing. Blessed be the Lord, forevermore! In Jesus, name, Amen.

And thine ears shall hear a word behind thee, saying, This is the way, walk ye in it, when ye turn to the right hand, and when ye turn to the left. Isaiah 30:21^{KJV}

Notes

Week 40

•••

RESTORE MY FASTING LIFE

As they ministered to the Lord, and fasted, the Holy Ghost said, Separate me Barnabas and Saul for the work whereunto I have called them. Acts 13:2^{KJV}

Maybe fasting was once a large part of your life, but things changed, and now you don't know where to start. Your fasting life has diminished-given a lack of will-power and self-control, as the spirit of gluttony has taken over in its place. You may have found it challenging to say no to food, or you may have experienced fatigue and excruciating headaches when fasting. This made it difficult to sustain the fast for the designated period. Have you encountered days when you did not consciously fast but didn't eat the entire day, and you experienced no headaches or discomfort?

Beloved, your fasting life is under siege by Satan. He understands the power and benefits of fasting and praying. Thus, he will do anything he can to prevent the growth of your fasting life. He knows your fasting and prayer is a sophisticated weapon that will paralyze demonic assignments, override principalities, destroy powers, and possibly raise the dead. I challenge you to strengthen your relationship with the Lord by restoring your fasting sessions. Start by playing some gospel music. Be sure to read the Word. Psalm chapters 8 and 121 are two great chapters to read and use as a focal point for your prayer, if you are one who believes you cannot or do not know how to pray. Praying the Words of God back to Him is an excellent way to build your prayer-life and your arsenal of weaponry. Also, you may take a visit to YouTube and listen to some uplifting sermons. Fasting, without praying and reading the Word can be considered a hunger strike.

Week 40 - Restore My Fasting Life

My friend, condition your mind to make a difference in the lives of those who are afflicted with natural or demonic infirmities. I command your spirit man to rise and take control of your flesh. There are situations around you which need to be addressed-strongholds that need to be broken- and demons that require restraint. You are a mighty tool in the hand of God. Restore your fasting life and allow Him to use you, mightily.

Fasting will allow God to set you apart for His use.

Prayer

Dear Heavenly Father,

Bless the Lord, O my soul, and all that is within me, bless His holy name. I honor You, O Sovereign King. How majestic is Your name in all the earth. Master, I praise and exalt Your holy name.

El Selichot, the one who forgives, please forgive me for yielding to my flesh and disobeying Your instruction. Father God, forgive me for neglecting You. Lord, I repent for my rebelliousness. Please forgive me. O Mighty God, I surrender my heart, mind, and soul to You.

Almighty God, endow me with the power to say no to food when it's time to fast. Elohim, I ask that You would restore my fasting life so I will be equipped to loose bands of wickedness, undo heavy burdens, free the oppressed, break and destroy every yoke, in the mighty name of Jesus. Master, when Your disciples asked You why were they unable to cast out the demons out of the child, You answered, *Howbeit this kind goeth not out but by prayer and fasting*. Abba Father, please restore my fasting-life so I can be effective during the deliverance process for those who are bound and tormented by foul spirits.

In the mighty name of Jesus, I use the weapon of fasting to pull down and destroy the stronghold of gluttony, greed, evil counsel, demonic sabotage, and confusion. Father God, with great expectation, I look forward to the restoration of my fasting life so I can once again experience the yoke destroying anointing, that will cause demons and devils to abandon their assignments, and rendered powerless, in Jesus' mighty name.

Holy Spirit, teach me how to minister to the Lord and how to fast, effectively, in Jesus' name. Awesome God, set me apart for Your use, as You did with Barnabas and Saul. Teach me the discipline of fasting that will restore my spiritual hearing and discernment, in Jesus' name. Open my ears, O God to hear Your voice and the plots of the enemy. Holy Spirit, activate my hunger for fasting, strengthen my spirit-man, and water my soul, in the mighty name of Jesus.

Adonai, thank You for restoring my life of fasting. I thank You for liberating my soul. Thank You for restoring my zeal for prayer and fasting. Most of all, thank You for not leaving nor forsaking me. Blessed be the Lord, forevermore! In Jesus' name, Amen.

Thus saith the Lord, the Holy One of Israel, and his Maker, Ask me of things to come concerning my sons, and concerning the work of my hands command ye me Isaiah 45:11^{KJV}

Notes

Week 41

•••

RESTORE MY COMMITMENT

That is why I am suffering as I am. Yet this is no cause for shame, because I know whom I have believed, and am convinced that he is able to guard what I have entrusted to him until that day.
2 Timothy 1:12^{NIV}

Are you missing out on the finer things in life because you lost the spirit of commitment? Lacking commitment means you no longer fulfill your promises. You forfeit agreements, and you don't keep your word. Let's explore the following to see if you can identify in which area you may be lacking commitment.

Physical Commitment

If you are no longer willing to share your life with your spouse, you have lost the commitment to your marriage. If you keep secrets from each other, the promise you made to be honest is broken. If your behavior becomes more reserved, it reflects an unwillingness to be open and transparent.

You may also lose the commitment to your job. One indication of this is that you arrive to work late and consistently desire to leave sooner than expected. Also, you no longer try to exceed expectations, and you consider quitting before finding a solution when challenges arise. Further, you may have lost commitment to yourself. You stop the pursuit of your dreams and visions, relinquish self-care and personal hygiene routines, and neglect other important areas in your life.

Week 41 - Restore My Commitment

Spiritual Commitment

Lacking spiritual commitment will interfere with your faith, belief, trust, and your love for God. Your faith will begin to waver and leave you dependent upon yourself to make decisions. You question what you once believed, and you no longer trust God to perform miracles. Further, you spend more time devoted to people and things, above spending time with God, which demonstrates a strain in your love for Him. As humans, we are naturally prone to commitment. Hence, without a spiritual connection to God, commitment and attention can waver to other things besides God, Himself.

Beloved, during these perilous days, if your commitment to God is not anchored securely, you may stray from God for the sake of earthy gain or the comfort of your flesh. Where and with whom does your loyalty lie? Commitment requires dedication and obligation to the person with whom you are connected. When you are in a spiritual relationship with God, you are obligated to contribute to the strengthening of that bond, despite hardship. In fact, commitment and dedication to God are even more important during times of hardship. It was Daniel's commitment to God that made him continue to pray despite the signed decree to punish anyone who worshipped a god other than the king.

It was Pauls' commitment to God that propelled him to write Romans chapter 8 and emphasized the depth of his love, determination, and loyalty for his Savior in verses 37-39. It was Jesus' commitment to the Father and to us that made him say, *And he went a little further, and fell on his face, and prayed, saying, O my Father, if it be possible, let this cup pass from me: nevertheless not as I will, but as thou wilt. Matthew 26:39*^{KJV}. Given Jesus' dedication to His mission, He bore the excruciating pain to set you and me free from Hell. Fulfilling your commitment speaks highly of your character, as it builds your integrity. Remaining committed to the Holy Spirit, you will be endowed with power, as it enhances your anointing, refuels your fire, builds your confidence, protects your mind, and encourages you to grow your faith.

Stay committed so you can stay connected.

Prayer

Dear Heavenly Father,

I praise You for all You've done for me. I honor You. I adore you. Precious Lord, You are everything to me. O how sweet it is to lean and depend on You. I Love You, Lord.

Elohim, the mighty God, I confess, I have not been fully committed to Your ways. I forfeit all that I have committed to you. Father God, I have compromised my dedication and salvation and pledged allegiance to another, out of fear. Lord, please forgive me for not trusting You enough to stay committed, regardless of the threat and intimidation. Forgive me, O, God, for allowing others to negatively influence my commitment to you, in Jesus' name.

In the mighty name of Jesus, I ask that You restore my spiritual and physical commitment. Father, I rededicate my life, and I renew my commitment to You, in Jesus' name. Today, I choose to learn from this mistake, as I place my loyalty and devotion back to You, in Jesus name. Almighty God, I recommit my mind, heart, body, and soul, to You, in Jesus' name. I recommit my finances, business, family, health, child/ children in Your loving arms, in Jesus mighty name. Lord, I recommit all that I do in Your hands. Thank You for establishing them.

Jehovah Melphati, the God who delivers, in the mighty name of Jesus, I use the weapons of devotedness to pull down and bind up the strongholds of intimidation, fear, compromise, and inconsistency out of my life. Father God, with the power vested in me, I firmly stand and declare as Paul did in Romans 8:37-39, *Nay, in all these things we are more than conquerors through him that loved us.* [38]*For I am persuaded, that neither death, nor life, nor angels, nor principalities, nor powers, nor things present, nor things to come,*[3] [9]*Nor height, nor depth, nor any other creature, shall be able to separate us from the love of God, which is in Christ Jesus our Lord.* All-powerful God, I declare and decree that no lack, joblessness, illness, persecution, disease, virus, or vaccine will make me give-in or compromise Your promise and lose my commitment to You, in Jesus' name.

Thank You, Lord, for restoring my commitment and covenant with You. Blessed be the Lord, forevermore! In Jesus' name. Amen.

Commit to the Lord whatever you do, and he will establish your plans. Proverbs 16:3^{NIV}

DAILY RESTORATIONAL

Notes

Week 42

•••

RESTORE MY CONSISTENCY

Let us hold unswervingly to the hope we profess, for he who promised is faithful. Hebrews 10:23^{NIV}

Inconsistency can be detrimental to our Christian journey. Irregularity can cost us our anointing and diminishes our power. In what areas of your life have you identified the most inconsistency? Is it during the management of a business? Is it in your relationship with God? Most of us are inconsistent, both physically and spiritually, especially in our relationships with God. For instance, when we feel most led by the spirit, we prioritize time to read our bibles and pray relentlessly. Further, we attend regularly scheduled fasting services and bible studies.

However, following our "holy high", bible reading suddenly becomes less appealing, and other duties take priority over fasting. Previously scheduled prayer times are forgotten, and before you know it, days and weeks have passed without us reading a verse from a chapter or engaging in deep worship or spirit-filled prayer.

Beloved, Daniel could have given up after waiting so long for his prayers to be answered, but because he knew the character of God, he **continued** to pray until his blessings were revealed. He remained consistent in prayer, regardless. Though you have not yet seen or received the blessings or breakthroughs you are praying for, do not give up. Be relentless, and determine, to remain connected to God, the Creator of the universe, despite the obstacles, setbacks, and delays. Be aware of the spiritual warfare that surrounds you; fight with all your might and to be victorious.

To remain consistent, you should set attainable goals; accept your imperfection and keep striving for the best, encourage yourself with positive words only, erase negative words from your vocabulary, create a vision board, stay clear of distractions, don't be afraid to ask for help, recognize your strength and embrace your weakness.

When you are consistent and refuse to compromise, Satan has no choice but to tremble when you get down on your knees to pray.

The enemy of your soul is consistent and persistent. Satan does not get weary, and he will never quit. His goal is to wear you down with shame, disappointment, and other negative thoughts until you give up on your Godly relationship. My friend, this is not the time to get lazy, relaxed, or weaken in your faith. You must be persistent with your devotion to God, for laziness can cause inconsistency. *Lazy hands make for poverty, but diligent hands bring wealth. Proverbs 10:4^{NIV}*

Being consistent is the key to victory.

Prayer

Dear Heavenly Father,

Thank You for being an unchanging God. You are forever deserving of my praise and worship. Thank You for being the same today, yesterday, and forever.

Heavenly Father, help me to avoid walking in the spirit of inconsistency. Help me not to be a quitter but to follow through with everything that I have started. Master, I confess, that inconsistency has caused me to be spiritually malnourished. Elohim, inconsistency has prevented me from reaching my full potential. It has hindered my gifts from reaching maturity and manifesting in their season. Father, the lack of consistency has robbed me of great opportunities and

WEEK 42 - RESTORE MY CONSISTENCY

prevented me from walking in my calling. It has hindered me many times from receiving the victory; and as a result, I became the victim. O mighty God, please hear my heart's cry for Your help. Father, I ask that you restore the spirit of consistency in my life.

El Shaddai, I am reminded in Your Word, that You are the all-sufficient God, the God that does not change. And You are not a man that You should lie, neither the son of man that You should repent. O, Covenant keeping God, I know You will not break Your covenant or alter any word that is gone out of Your mouth. Help me to follow Your pattern of consistency, in Jesus' mighty name.

Abba Father, in the mighty name of Jesus, I use the weapon of persistence to pull down and bind up the stronghold of procrastination, inconsistency, laziness, neglectfulness, inactivity, sluggishness, and self-sabotage. With the power of the Holy Spirit, I release the spirit of endurance, perseverance, consistency, and activeness in my life, as I exemplify the spirit of Christ, in Jesus' mighty name.

Almighty God, I desire to be consistent in my words, thoughts, and actions. Lord, thank You for restoring my ability to be consistent in every area of my life. Blessed be the Lord, forevermore! In Jesus' name, Amen.

Therefore, my dear brothers and sisters, stand firm. Let nothing move you. Always give yourselves fully to the work of the Lord, because you know that your labor in the Lord is not in vain. 1 Corinthians 15:58^{NIV}

Notes

Week 43

•••

Restore My Focus

Looking unto Jesus the author and finisher of our faith; who for the joy that was set before him endured the cross, despising the shame, and is set down at the right hand of the throne of God.
Hebrews 12:2^{KJV}

There are so many things competing for your physical and spiritual attention, whether it is on social media, in the home, at church, on the job, or even in your quiet time, alone. Did you know that secular activities and church activities can interfere with your focus, causing you to shift priority and lose a sense of direction? It is possible to be busy but not productive, given your priority is out of focus. It is evident that, if you do too many things at the same time, you will never give your best to any one thing.

Have you noticed that when you read or pray, your mind wanders off on irrelevant things? That's because your focus is out of alignment. Also, if you find that people ignore you when you speak, check to see if you jump from one subject to the next during your conversations. Bring structure to your thoughts. Losing focus can detour you from the right path and delay your progress, physically and spiritually.

There is chaos all around you. This is not the time to lose focus, for if you lack focus or a sense of direction, you will be swept away in the current of confusion. Wake up, straighten your lens, prioritize, stay alert, and be watchful. Keep your eyes fastened on Jesus. If you find yourself getting distracted and unable to stay focused, get in the presence of God; be still while you meditate on His Word, His promises, His character, and His attributes. If you meditate on God continuously, He promises that you will be like a tree planted by the rivers of water that brings forth fruits in its season, and the leaves shall not wither.

Satan desires to see you confused, frustrated, miserable, and stagnant. Remember, distractions can come in all forms and from unexpected places. Stay connected and focused on the goal in mind, irrespective of the hindrances. I implore you, don't allow yourself to be distracted or weaved into the web of busyness, for you may miss your real purpose. Overly activating the mind and coming up with good ideas can pose as a distraction as well. Whenever you are presented with a good idea, always seek the direction of the Holy Spirit. You want to know for sure whether it's your idea or if it's a God idea.

Beloved, do not allow the giant, the red sea, the fiery furnace, the lion, or the den, make you lose focus. The COVID-19 pandemic has come as a distraction, and because of life's uncertainty, fear has paralyzed many, causing them to lose focus. These are the last days Jesus spoke about. It is all written in your Bible, so I urge you to open it and start searching for the plans of God for us during this time. Men purposed in their hearts to destroy the human race, especially those who refuse to bow to their ways of life or compromise their salvation. Please, condition your mind that no matter what persecution comes upon you, make Jesus the center of your focus.

Stand your ground as, the three Hebrew boys, Paul, Stephen, and Daniel did for God. Although death for them seemed certain, they refused to give-in or bow to any other god or idols. Instead, they focused on God and remained committed and dedicated to His sovereignty and were willing to die for Him. When Stephen was being stoned, he did not lose focus. Acts 7:55-56 reads, *But he, being full of the Holy Ghost, looked up steadfastly into heaven, and saw the glory of God, and Jesus standing on the right hand of God* **Behold, I see the heavens opened, and the Son of man standing on the right hand of God.**

Week 43 - Restore My Focus

I beg you, keep your eyes on the Author and finisher of your faith. Trust the one who will make you live again, even after your flesh dies. I command your focus to be restored now, in Jesus' name.

> Amidst the chaos, ask God to restore and redirect your focus, so you will not be caught off guard.

Prayer

Dear Heavenly Father,

Thank You for being my Shepherd and for providing everything I need. I worship You and give You all the glory and honor. You are my rock, my helper, and my refuge.

Jehovah Go'el, my redeemer, thank You for redeeming me from all my sins. Lord, I have lost focus. Forgive me for allowing myself to be distracted and allowing the enemy to distract me. Forgive me for allowing myself to be blinded by the schemes and plots of the wicked one. Forgive me for not being sober and watchful. Father, wash and cleanse me, with Your blood, from all unrighteousness, sinful thoughts, and deeds, in Jesus' name.

Father, I ask that You restore my focus, in Jesus' name. Almighty God, help me to keep my eyes on You, alone. Jehovah Magen, You are my shield. Shield me from any ungodly distractions. Give me perfect peace amidst the chaos. I declare that my focus will forever be fixed on You, in Jesus' mighty name. Father God, thank You for drawing close to me as I draw close to You, in Jesus' name.

In the mighty name of Jesus, I use the weapon of alertness to pull down and destroy the stronghold of distraction, double-mindedness, and confusion. Jehovah Mephalti, deliver my mind from the conspiracy of all evil counsel and demonic sabotage. Send Michael, Your warrior angel to arrest them along with the spirit of confusion and frustration, in Jesus' mighty name. Lord, with great expectation, I look forward to the restoration of my focus so that I will be vigilant in every area of my life.

Through the power in the blood of Jesus, I cancel every assignment, assigned to draw my focus away from God, in Jesus' name. I declare that I will remain alert, and keep my focus on the things that are true, honorable, right, pure, lovely, and of good report.

Blessed be the Lord, forevermore! In Jesus' name, Amen.

Set your mind and keep focused habitually on the things above [the heavenly things], not on things that are on the earth [which have only temporal value]. Colossians 3:2 ^{AMP}

Notes

Week 44

•••

RESTORE MY ZEAL

For zeal for your house consumes me, and the insults of those who insult you fall on me. Psalm 69:9 ^{NIV}

*D*o you stay awake at night or feel restless when you realize you lost your passion for being in the presence of God? Do you feel discouraged when you reflect on how enthusiastic and willing you once were to tell someone about Jesus and His saving grace? Whereas, now you have no zeal to spread the good news and lift His name in reverence or spend personal time with Him. The past cannot be changed, therefore, don't overly criticize or question yourself regarding what you should or should not have done. Embrace the present and strive to have an excellent future. *Brothers and sisters, I do not consider myself yet to have taken hold of it. But one thing I do: Forgetting what is behind and straining toward what is ahead. Philippians 3:13^{NIV}*

If you feel discouraged about your past, use it as a reason to be re-energized and motivated to restore your zeal. Get up and run the race set before you. *Wherefore seeing we also are compassed about with so great a cloud of witnesses, let us lay aside every weight, and the sin which doth so easily beset us, and let us run with patience the race that is set before us. Hebrews 12:1^{KJV}.*

Beloved, witness the calamity around you. People's faith, trust, and beliefs are no longer solid. There is great uproar all over the world, as people feel unsettled and depressed because of the unknown. Therefore, this is the time to rise, be motivated to minister, and spread the news about the sincere love of Jesus Christ. Their hearts are ready, so don't miss this opportunity. There is a real enemy at work, seeking who he may devour and whose minds he can manipulate. You can get your zeal back and change your position in Christ by, first, being hungry and thirsty enough to surrender your thoughts to Him. De-clutter your mind from the cares of this world. Refuse to worry about the situations you cannot change, and trust God to handle them. Perhaps, you have never allowed Him to be in full control of your life and affairs; therefore, you are unaware of His capabilities. I command the enthusiasm, eagerness, zeal, and motivation to spend time with God and do His work be restored unto you right now, in Jesus' name.

Build God an altar. Set aside a secret place to meet with Him, daily.

Prayer

Dear Heavenly Father,

I welcome You into my life. You are the omnipotent Father, full of mercy and grace. I worship and adore You. (Beloved, take a few minutes right here and worship God).

Jehovah Bara, Creator of the Universe, I bow in humility before Your throne of mercy. Have mercy on me, O God, and cleanse me from sin, shame, and disgrace. Jehovah Hoshe'ah, You saved me from Hell and spiritual death, yet, I tried to ignore and reject the unction of the Holy Spirit to prayer, praise, and worship. God, forgive me for taking You for granted.

Abba Father, I admit that I have lost my zeal to work for You, spend time in your presence, and even to share You with others. Please, forgive me, in Jesus' name. I repent for taking You for granted and neglecting my commission to go to the highway and hedges. Father, forgive me for ignoring the souls who needed to be encouraged to seek You and Your kingdom first.

In the mighty name of Jesus, I use the weapon of zeal to pull down the stronghold of lackadaisicalness, halfheartedness, and laziness. Father God, with the weapon of devotedness and enthusiasm, I destroy every evil counsel, demonic sabotage, and spirit of frustration that interfered with my passion for You and Your work, in Jesus' mighty name. Adonai, with great expectation, I look forward to the restoration of my zeal to worship, witness, encourage, and empower others, in Jesus' name.

El Yeshuati, God of my salvation, I ask that You will restore my zeal, in Jesus' name. O mighty God, restore my enthusiasm to spend adequate time in Your Word. In the mighty name of Jesus, restore my zeal to seek Your face multiple times per day, linger in Your presence, and discover Your perfect will for my life. Almighty God, restore my desire to serve You with gladness. Thank You, Adonai, I can feel my zeal restoring. Thank You for the restoration. Blessed be the Lord, forevermore! In Jesus' name, Amen.

And he said unto him, Lord, I am ready to go with thee, both into prison, and to death. Luke 22:33^{KJV}

Notes

Week 45

•••

RESTORE MY RESPECT

Respect everyone, and love the family of believers. Fear God, and respect the king. 1 Peter 2:17 NLT

We constantly witness children who have lost respect for their parents and teachers. We witness spouses who have lost respect for each other, employees who have lost respect for employers, members who have lost respect for their pastors, and individuals who have lost self-respect. Unbelievably, many lose respect for God.

When one has integrity, they often care more about how their spouse, friends, and children feel when one hurts their feelings, but they feel less guilty when they offend God. We quickly honor others for a job well done. Therefore, men are held in high esteem, and there is no restraint regarding the appreciation and admiration we show for someone with unique abilities, exceptional qualities, and excellent achievements.

Respect is due to everyone, and honor should be given to all who are deserving. There is nothing wrong with this. However, God must feel insulted when men are exalted over Him. We have lost respect for God, His teachings, and His Sovereignty, and, as a result, we live forbidden lifestyles. We prefer to hide our wrongdoings from a man but, presumptuously, perform them openly before God. We are tactful with our language around specific individuals, however, we curse and swear, in the presence of God, as if He doesn't get offended. Further, we temper our anger and bad attitudes with man, but we disregard God's opinions and lose integrity when expressing our emotions.

Week 45 - Restore My Respect

Beloved, seek to restore your respect for God, immediately. Otherwise, without reservation, you will readily accept the negative things in your life as if they belong. Losing respect for God is the same as losing the fear of God. If your conscience doesn't convict you when you break His commandments, and you are not afraid of the consequences for your contrary actions, this means you have lost respect for God. Whoever has taken the place of God's reverence, can they help or deliver you from the snares of the enemy?

Make God your priority.

Prayer

Dear Heavenly Father,

I bless and praise Your name. You are worthy and holy. I magnify Your name because You are the lover of my soul.

Father God, forgive me for treating You as if I have arrived and I am operating independently of You. Father, I have sinned against You by disrespecting You, Your Word, and others. Father God, I am guilty of trespassing against others and transgressing against Your law. I repent for disrespecting, displeasing, and dishonoring You and not being concerned about the consequences. Lord, please forgive me, in Jesus' name.

Father, in the name of Jesus, I ask that You restore my respect, so I may walk in obedience to Your Word. Mighty God, in the name of Jesus, I ask that You restore my respect and reverence for Your presence. El Elyon, restore my respect so I can honor and appreciate the works of Your mighty hands. God of compassion, in the name of Jesus, I desire to rebuild a relationship with You. Please, do not turn away from me.

In the mighty name of Jesus, I use the weapon of honor to pull down and destroy the stronghold of disrespect, dishonor, irreverence, and bad attitude. Lord, with great anticipation, I look forward to the restoration of my reverence for You. Abba Father, restore unto me the kind of respect that will make me bow in humility before You, stand in awe in Your presence, and marvel at the works of Your hands.

Lord, thank You for loving me despite my disrespectful behavior. Thank You for Your patience towards me, and thank You for not giving me what I deserve. Master, thank You for another opportunity to align my life with Your words, in Jesus' name. O God, restore my covenant with You as I esteem You above everything and everyone, in Jesus mighty name. Blessed be the Lord, forevermore! In Jesus' name, Amen.

I will look on you with favor and make you fruitful and increase your numbers, and I will keep my covenant with you. Leviticus 26:9[NIV]

Notes

Week 46

•••

Restore My Peace

These things I have spoken to you, that in me ye may have peace. In the world ye shall have tribulation, but be of good cheer; I have overcome the world. John 16:33^{KJV}

Have you ever felt like the world around you was completely chaotic? When you are at home, you are miserable. When you are at work, it feels tormenting. When you are in church, it feels torturous. Have you ever been there? This feeling occurs because your peace is disturbed by the enemy of your soul. When peace is bothered, it impacts everything in your life and leaves you feeling frustrated and miserable.

Upon the arrival of the year 2020, we anticipated a perfect year, as it's been referred to as the year of "2020 vision," which is considered a perfect vision. However, here comes the pandemic. Now, the entire world is experiencing unsettled peace. Perhaps, you prayed relentlessly for the year to quickly come to its close because it is not as perfect as you thought it would. For many, the year brought sadness, death, sickness, loss of income, and loss of freedom; and so, many assume that when the year is past, so will their worries and problems. They firmly believe that situation will get better and there will be a great sense of peace. Unfortunately, peace is not found in a year, a person, or a thing. While you are waiting for the year to come to an end, peace may be passing you by. Our finite minds expect things to be done or given to us in the same way at all times; as a result, we may have missed out on a lot of blessings and favors because the packaging is different. Although the pandemic interrupts the peace of many individuals, there are those who kept their peace, and some found peace amid the unexplainable disturbance. Peace, like joy, is a choice, and it depends on what you choose.

Beloved, if you are one who believes, and is waiting for peace to come in the upcoming year, you are looking to the wrong source. Peace is one of the most incredible fruits of the spirit an individual can possess, but it grows from being connected to the Prince of Peace. Jesus is His name. Once you are connected to Him, rest assured that peace will always be with you where ever you go; no matter the situation, you will never be alone. If your peace comes from another source other than God, you may be in trouble; if you are disobedient or unfaithful to that other source, they have the power to pull the plug and take your peace off life support, leaving you in conflict. Jesus will give you the peace that no man can take away, no arrow can penetrate, no pandemic can interrupt, and no government can order it to stay home, or observe social distancing. My friend, your boat may be caught during a storm, but peace is on-board, just call Him. Peace is activated in imperfect situations. Being connected to the Prince of Peace doesn't negate the fact that unseen danger will arise, but it's during those imperfect times when your perfect peace will be made manifest.

Don't insist on getting everything right or in perfect order before you can embrace peace. You may have heard the sayings, "I am a perfectionist" Or, "I have a type-A personality, I have to get things done a certain way" Or, " I have OCD (obsessive-compulsive disorder)." These individuals may never find inner peace. When they should be relaxing, they are being anxious and sweating the small stuff. God is the only one who can do everything perfectly well because He is perfect. Resist the peace stealer, and he will flee. It is time to claim victory and command the restoration of your peace. Seek not the peace of man or the peace of this world but the peace of God, which gives you comfort and settles your frame of mind, making you more understanding and tolerant of others, even in the most disturbing situations. Once again, Jesus is your peace during your storm, He is your Prince of Peace, He is your bridge over troubled waters, and He is your peace in the fire.

You may not experience real peace if you are constantly worrying about the things that you can't change. Rest in God, no matter the situation, for He has your back. Let go and let God!

Prayer

Dear Heavenly Father,

Thank You for being my peace. I rejoice in You because You care for me. Father, forgive me for allowing fear, worry, and anxiety to consume my heart. I admit, I took my eyes off of You and placed my focus and trust in people and circumstances. Lord, I surrender my mind, body, and soul to You, today. Give me Your peace that surpasses all understanding.

In the mighty name of Jesus, I use the weapon of peace to pull down and destroy the stronghold of worry, anxiety, restlessness, and frustration. In the name of Jesus, with great anticipation, I look forward to the restoration of my peace. You are my everlasting Prince of Peace that will guard my heart and mind through Jesus Christ. Lord, as my peace is restored in You, I ask that You would give me a calm spirit to be still in the midst of chaotic situations, in Jesus' name. Jehovah Shalom, grant me the kind of peace that will make me confident, knowing that You are God, and You have the whole world in Your hands, in Jesus' name. O, mighty God, You are the only source of real peace.

El Shaddai, all-sufficient God, I will not be anxious for anything, but in everything by prayer and supplication and with thanksgiving, I will let my requests be made known to You. James 3:18 says peacemakers who sow in peace reap a harvest of righteousness. God, help me to be the peacemaker who will continue to sow peace, in Jesus' name.

Week 46 - Restore My Peace

Hallelujah. God, may You continue to wrap Your arms around me and keep my mind in perfect peace. Lord, give me Your peace that will allow me to understand beyond what my natural eyes can see, in Jesus' name. O, Mighty God of Zion, as a carrier of Your peace, help me to live peaceably with all men. Help me to release, in Your hands, the things that I cannot control, in Jesus' name.

Jehovah Shalom, my peace, thank You for giving me peace that surpasses all my understanding. Thank You for Your peace that compels me to turn from evil and do good. Thank You for Your peace that allows me to seek peace and pursue it, and rest in Your presence, in Jesus' name. God of peace, thank You for peace at home, peace in the church, peace amongst friends, and peace on the job, in Jesus' name. By faith, I receive the restoration of my peace. Blessed be the Lord, forevermore! In Jesus' name, Amen.

Cast all your anxiety on him because he cares for you. 1 Peter 5:7[NIV]

Notes

Week 47

•••

RESTORE MY JOY

Looking unto Jesus the author and finisher of our faith; who for the joy that was set before him endured the cross, despising the shame, and is set down at the right hand of the throne of God.

Hebrews 12:2KJV

There is a vast difference between happiness and joy. Joy is a choice, and it is permanent, while happiness is temporary. It is possible to have happiness and lack joy, but once you have joy, happiness is guaranteed. For instance, you may have heard someone say, "If I get married, I will be so happy" or, "I know I will be happy if I get my dream job, dream house, and dream car." Some believe winning the lottery will make them happy. All of the statements can be true because happiness depends on tangible things and present circumstances. Additionally, one can experience a dark moment in their life and feel sad, but when they get into the company of friends, their smiles and laughter are restored, and they genuinely enjoy themselves because they are having fun. However, after that moment is over, they return to sadness. Hence, happiness is temporary.

Joy stems from having a solid relationship with God. Joy is the manifestation of your faith, peace, hope, trust, and patience being anchored in God. When you are anchored in Christ, you are not bothered by large or small issues. You could face multiple tribulations, both at work and at home, and you manage to remain calm and maintain your smile. This is the epitome of joy. This demonstrates that joy does not depend on tangible items or present circumstances. Instead, joy derives from an inner peace of knowing who you are, and who lives on the inside of you. The joy of the Lord will make you feel compassion for individuals who hurt you. Rather than perceiving them in a negative light, you will view them as helpless and needing peace and deliverance from their inner turmoil.

Beloved, you may be in pain, but there is an inner peace knowing that your sorrow will not last. Your faith will remind you that God is with you, and you will not fail. Perhaps the bills are piled up, but hope will ensure you that Jehovah Jireh will provide and make a way of escape from debt. The doctor's report may not be favorable, but with trust abound, God will deliver you from affliction. You may be anxious to succeed but get discouraged because of delays and setbacks. Patience encourages you not to worry, for waiting on the Lord will renew your strength. Do not rely on your own understanding, but instead, acknowledge God, and He will direct your path. The joy of the Lord is permanent. Don't allow the trials and challenges of life to steal your joy, and be sure to anchor your joy in the Lord.

Joy is experienced by anticipating a positive result despite the doom and gloom that is hovering on the horizon. Jesus was disgraced and openly shamed, and though He was in excruciating pain, He remembered for whom He came to Earth. He knew that, despite the turmoil, He would experience an unspeakable joy for us not having to reign with Satan in a place of torment. Nehemiah 8:10 attests that the joy of the Lord is your strength, therefore, we should strive to be in the presence of God where joy overflows. Without joy, you are being deprived of your best life. Without the joy of the Lord, you are only existing and not living. However, you can start to live when you command your joy and laughter to be restored unto you.

Now the God of hope fill you with all joy and peace in believing, that ye may abound in hope through the power of the Holy Ghost. Romans 15:3

May your joy be anchored in Jesus Christ, the only begotten Son God.

Prayer

Dear Heavenly Father,

I love You, I adore You, and I glorify Your name in all the Earth. I praise You for this day. This is the day You have made, and in it, I will rejoice and be glad.

El Gibbor, the mighty God, please forgive me for allowing the enemy to tamper with my Joy. Omniscient Father, I humbly ask that You forgive me for walking out of Your presence where there is fulness of joy. Lord, forgive me for not trusting and believing that Your joy is my strength. Forgive me for allowing the cares of life and other obligations to weigh me down to the point where I can't experience Your joy. O mighty God, forgive me for allowing anger and unforgiveness to consume my heart and steal my joy. Lord, I ask that You would restore unto me the spirit of joy.

In the mighty name of Jesus, I use the weapon of joy to pull down and destroy the stronghold of sadness, discouragement, discomfort, tribulation, and misery. Father God, with great expectation, I look forward to the restoration of my joy, in Jesus' mighty name. Lord, I am extremely grateful for the restoration of my joy.

Adonai, thank You for restoring unto me the joy of my salvation. Thank You that Your joy is my strength. Master, today, I give You all the glory and praise because I can reject depression, sorrow, worry, and fear, and I receive the fullness of Your joy, in Jesus' name. God. Lord, I will continue to give You thanks for Your goodness and Your mercy which endures forever. Blessed be the Lord, forevermore! In Jesus' name, Amen.

And those the Lord has rescued will return. They will enter Zion with singing; everlasting joy will crown their heads. Gladness and joy will overtake them, and sorrow and sighing will flee away. Isaiah 35:10^{NIV}

Daily Restorational

Notes

_____ *Week 48*

•••
Restore My Hope

Now the God of hope fill you with all JOY and peace in believing, that ye may abound in hope, through the power of the Holy Ghost.
Romans 15:13^{KJV}

Where, and on whom is your hope built? Job exhibited incredible hope, because during his tribulations, he trusted and exercised faith in God, despite wishing to be delivered from his pain. I encourage you to read the entire book of Job to get a scope of his story of faith.

The book of Daniel, chapter three shares how Shadrach, Meshach, and Abednego trusted and believed that God would rescue them from the burning furnace. They hoped in God's deliverance power.

Elijah, after he slew over four hundred men, ran and hid from Jezebel. She could not find him, but God did. Although he was afraid and wanted to die, his hope in God illuminated when God provided for him, daily. God ensured there was water to keep him hydrated, food to sustain him, as well as, both the juniper tree and cave, to protect him from the elements. This story is found in 1 Kings, chapter 19.

When Jeremiah was thrown into the mud-filled dungeon and was sinking, he hoped in God for his rescue. This story is found in Jeremiah, chapter 38.

Joseph was thrown into the pit by his brothers, then removed and sold into slavery. He then acquired a job, and while there, he was falsely accused and thrown into prison. Despite his ill-luck, he hoped in God for a breakthrough, which he received, unlimitedly. His story began in Genesis 37-50

In the aforementioned stories, everyone was blessed. Their hope was anchored in the assurance that God could deliver them from any desperate situation. By faith, they waited and trusted God, and they were delivered. Where there is no hope, defeat and despair take refuge. Men do not manufacture hope, but God does, and that is the only hope that will sustain you through tumultuous times. *The Lord delights in those who fear him, who put their hope in his unfailing love. Psalm 147:11^{NIV}*

Beloved, you may feel hopeless like there is no solution to your problems. However, because you are alive, there will always be hope, as God has a plan for your life. Perhaps you feel desperate, discouraged, and disappointed, which makes you feel empty. Place your hope in God. Don't allow your circumstances to encourage you to seek other gods or elicit help from other sources. When one becomes hopeless, they are vulnerable and often incline their ears to anyone or anything which resembles hope, regardless if it is the truth. *If in this life only we have hope in Christ, we are of all men most miserable. 1 Corinthians 15:19^{KJV}*

If you don't know which way to turn, be still! Seek God first before you make a regretful decision. When you are unsure or confused, that is the optimal time to activate your faith and trust Him. God doesn't have to tell you or show you everything He does on your behalf. If He did, you would have nothing to hope for nor would you need faith. While you wait for God, be productive, and use the gifts and talents with which you were entrusted. Maximize your current situation before He brings His plans for you to fruition. God is working things out in your favor, behind the scenes. Hoping in God is not futile, for men do not have the final say. When you seek God, you will find Him, and if you search for Him with all of your heart,

He will answer you. You must allow Him to be the only God in your life. *For I know the plans I have for you, declares the Lord, plans to prosper you and not to harm you, plans to give you hope and a future. Jeremiah 29:11*^{NIV}

The prospect of the righteous is joy, but the hopes of the wicked come to nothing. Proverbs 10:28 ^{NIV}

Prayer

Dear Heavenly Father,

I praise You because You are lovely and marvelous. Holy is Your name, Lord. You are my hope of glory. You are my hiding place and my shield, for I hope in Your Word. Spirit of the living God, fall afresh on me. Melt me, mold me, and fill me so that You can use me as a vessel of honor. Hallelujah. Prince of Peace, I just want to honor You because You are worthy of my praise.

El Elyon, the most high God, I ask Your forgiveness for walking in hopelessness and despair. Jesus, the magnificent fountain of hope, forgive me for doubting Your ability to bring forth the plans You have for me. Forgive me for placing my hope in anyone or anything else but You. Father, I ask that You restore my hope, in Jesus' name. O, merciful God, You are the motivation of my heart in times of despair. Lord, without hope, my life is futile.

In the mighty name of Jesus, I use the weapon of hope to pull down and destroy the stronghold of despair, despondency, and disbelief. Lord, with great anticipation, I look forward to the restoration of my hope, in Jesus' name. Sovereign God, You are my everlasting hope of glory. You are my hope for greater things to come, in Jesus' name. Lord, as my hope is restored in You, I ask that You would give me the fullness of joy, in Jesus name. I reject every whisper of defeat and despair, and I receive confidence and faith, in Jesus' name. I declare that I will place my hope in You, God, for You are the source of my strength.

Today, I make a conscious decision to seek You first and wait for You to bring to pass the plans You hold for my future. Thank You, Lord, for restoring my hope. Blessed be Your name, forevermore! In Jesus' name, Amen.

Have not I commanded thee? Be strong and of a good courage; be not afraid, neither be thou dismayed: for the Lord thy God is with thee whithersoever thou goest. Joshua 1:9^{KJV}

Notes

Week 49 _____

•••

Restore My Trust

Trust in the Lord with all your heart and lean not on your own understanding. Proverbs 3:5^{NIV}

How often have you heard the words, "Trust me?" Frequently, I'm sure. Without hesitation, most people are ready to place their trust in an individual. When someone asks for your trust, they are asking you to believe in and depend on them. Therefore, it is a shame when our trust is broken by those who compromise their integrity by being dishonest and disloyal.

You may have had disappointing experiences regarding friends or family members in whom you confided, loved, trusted, and for whom you cared. Even though they know that you were deeply affected by their deception and breach of trust, they never apologize or show any sign of remorse. Instead, they watched you suffer in agony, made excuses for their actions, moved heaven and earth to blame you, and sought to justify themselves.

Other individuals, by whom we may be deceived, are government administrators, religious officials, health industry professionals, and scientists. However, though we grieve the accompanying negative emotions, we forgive them and trust in them all over again. Why, then, is it so difficult to trust God? Above all else, God esteems His words above His name. He is not a man that He should lie or the son of man that He should repent. He will make good on His promises. You can always trust and depend on Him, in good or bad times.

Beloved, when you first heard of COVID-19 and the magnitude of its potential negative effects, what did you first consider? Did you practice social distancing? Did you close your business? Did you wear a mask and gloves as you were directed? If you answered yes to any of these questions, you adhered to the regulations because you believed in and were obedient to authorities. However, your decisions were gauged based on the assumption that authorities were telling the truth. Ultimately, you **trusted** these experts and **hoped** for the best. Therefore, can you trust God's Word the same way you trust the people in authority? Given that these authority figures were merely men, they didn't understand the extent of the trouble, however, they distributed instructions with the hope that they would keep people safe. This is evidence of our trust in mankind. Though we can't see God, we can feel His presence, and He asks that you trust Him. He is the only one who can see all and knows all.

When all else fails, you can always rely wholeheartedly on God. Humans are prone to disappoint and fail each other, but God, your Creator, will never disappoint you. Matthew 5:45^{KJV} reads, *"...for he maketh his sun to rise on the evil and on the good, and sendeth rain on the just and on the unjust."* In other words, even if you ignore, refuse, rebel against, and disobey God, He will still provide, protect, and pave the way for you. He didn't say you wouldn't get sick, but Psalm 147:3^{NIV} reads, *"He heals the brokenhearted and binds up their wounds."* God didn't promise you wouldn't have trouble, but He said in Psalm 50:15^{KJV}, *"And call upon me in the day of trouble: I will deliver thee, and thou shalt glorify me."* Therefore, He promises He will be with you, and no harm will come to you. *"When thou passest through the waters, I will be with thee; and through the rivers, they shall not overflow thee: when thou walkest through the fire, thou shalt not be burned; neither shall the flame kindle upon thee."* Isaiah 43:2^{KJV}. His promises are endless.

God is not surprised by anything. Beloved, whatever makes you anxious or afraid, God already knows about it, and He has a plan for your life. He will make sure you escape the grasps of those emotions without being harmed. An example of God's protective care is emphasized in the story of Daniel in the lion's den, found in the book of Daniel, chapter six. Do not forget, He is the same God who has saved you in the past. Do not try to analyze whether God is worthy of your trust. He deserves your trust and expects you to rely on His capacity to carry you through your challenges. Command your trust to be restored, and watch God move on your behalf. Prioritize God in your decision making, for He never fails. *Then Nebuchadnezzar said, Praise be to the God of Shadrach, Meshach and Abednego, who has sent his angel and rescued his servants! They trusted in him and defied the king's command and were willing to give up their lives rather than serve or worship any god except their own God. Daniel 3:28* ᴺᴵⱽ

You can't trace God, just trust Him.

Prayer

Dear Heavenly Father,

I adore You. I am crazy about You. I am grateful to You for being the lover of my soul. I appreciate You for being my protector, my mentor, my coach, my teacher, my comforter, and my revelator. I honor You.

El Selichot, the Lord who forgives. Forgive me for harboring unresolved hurt, pain, animosity, and resentment in my heart, in Jesus name. Uproot this darkness from within me, O God. Cleanse me thoroughly and deliver me from this iniquity in, Jesus' mighty name. Abba Father, please forgive me for entertaining the spirit of doubt and fear, in Jesus' name. Forgive me for placing my trust in man and not You. Lord, I have been wounded, repeatedly by so-called friends, family, co-workers, and even business colleagues.

Adonai, my Lord, and Master, I am comforted in knowing that the might of man cannot stand against Your glory, and the defeated foe cannot stand against the power You have given me. In the mighty name of Jesus, I use the weapon of trust to pull down the stronghold of doubt, skepticism, and mistrust, in Jesus' name. Lord, with great expectation, I look forward to the restoration of my trust.

Holy Spirit, help me not to lean on my own understanding but to acknowledge You in everything I do and say. Jehovah Mephalti, Lord My Deliverer, I place complete trust in You and not man. In the mighty name of Jesus, I place my trust in Jesus Christ and His blood but not vaccines. El Gibbor, the mighty God, I trust in Your salvation plan and not my retirement plan. Lord, I know You love and care for me beyond any human comprehension. Today, I commit my ways to You, in Jesus' name.

O Mighty God, if I am thrown into the fiery furnace, I will trust You. If I am thrown in the lion's den, I will trust You. If I am cast into a dungeon or a pot of oil, I will trust You. Father God, if I lose my job, home, car, or my family, I will trust You. Omniscient God, no matter how grim my circumstances are, I have no choice but to trust You. I trust You because You know what is best for me, in Jesus' name. Jehovah Mephalti, without a doubt, I am going to trust You with my heart, mind, body, and soul, in Jesus' name.

In the precious name of Jesus, I reject every spirit of fear, doubt, and intimidation that has caused me to mistrust You. Thank You, Lord, for restoring the spirit of trust within me. Thank You, Lord, for continuously watching over me, in Jesus' name. Thank You for fighting my battles. Blessed be the Lord, forevermore! Amen.

Therefore I tell you, do not worry about your life, what you will eat or drink; or about your body, what you will wear. Is not life more than food, and the body more than clothes? Matthew 6:25 NIV

Notes

Week 50

•••

RESTORE MY WORSHIP

Lord, you are my God; I will exalt you and praise your name, for in perfect faithfulness you have done wonderful things, things planned long ago. Isaiah 25:1 ^{NIV}

Worship is among one of the few things which will grab God's immediate attention. Sincere worship happens when you lose yourself in a spiritually charged atmosphere and surrender to God. Worship will cause God to change His mind on decisions already made. He will overturn life sentences and cancel death warrants. For instance, in Isaiah chapter 38, God sent Isaiah to tell Hezekiah to set his house in order because he was going to die. However, when Hezekiah turned his face to the wall and began to pray, God added fifteen years to Hezekiah's life.

Undiluted worship will transcend your faith experience. Unconditional adoration for God will open up the heavens on your behalf, and the angels will join you in worship. When you relinquish yourself to worship, nothing can distract or defeat you! Worship is one of our most powerful weapons in warfare, which is why Satan and his demons cannot interfere with sincere worship.

Beloved, if you want to become a worshiper, whose praise opens the heavens and touches the heart of God, I encourage you to limit your distractions from the outside world. When you eliminate the distractions and interlace with God, your hungry spirit will desire more of His delicacy and awesome power. To receive it, open your mouth and call forth the spirit of worship to be restored unto you.

Embrace the authenticity of His divinity through the power of worship and watch those stubborn obstacles get demolished. It is not a coincidence that you are reading this chapter right now. Your spirit man needs to worship. So, pause for a few minutes, engage yourself in worship and observe the destruction of challenging situations around you. Shut out the world and its baggage while you experience true worship, and let worship become a customary practice in your life. Praise is the railroad track on which your worship runs, and your worship is the faucet through which the anointing flows.

Prayer

Dear Heavenly Father,

I worship You in the splendor of holiness. I bow before You in worship. You alone are deserving of all of my worship, forever. I praise Your mighty name. Lord, You are magnificent. You are superb and excellent. I worship You for who You are. I give You praise, glory, and honor.

Elohim, the living God, please forgive me for taking each day for granted. Forgive me for not making worship a daily practice in my life. I repent for allowing the things of this world to take preeminence over my worship to You. Forgive me, Lord, for giving my worship to another, in Jesus' name.

In the mighty name of Jesus, I use the weapon of worship to pull down and destroy the stronghold of evil counsel, demonic sabotage, frustration, and confusion. Lord, with great expectation, I look forward to the restoration of sincere worship that pleases You, touches Your heart, and makes You smile. Adonai, restore unto me the kind of worship that will cramp and paralyze demons and devils.

Abba Father, I've come this far by faith, leaning on Your everlasting arms. Jehovah Yish'i, You are the horn of my salvation. In the precious name of Jesus, teach me how to worship in spirit and truth. Father, I ask that You restore unto me the spirit of worship. May the spirit of worship saturate me, quench the thirst of my soul, and feed my malnourished spirit.

Jehovah Immeku, the Lord is with me. You promise never to leave me nor forsake me. Teach me, Father God, how to worship You with a clean and pure heart, withholding nothing from You, in the name of Jesus. Master, I thank You for restoring unlimited worship in my life, home, and ministries, in Jesus' name. O mighty God, restore the kind of worship that cannot be diluted or penetrated by the arrows. Thank You, Jesus, for being the lover of my soul and the lifter of my head. Blessed be the Lord, forevermore! In Jesus' name, Amen.

Notes

_____ *Week 51*

•••
Restore My Praise

About midnight Paul and Silas were praying and singing hymns to God, and the other prisoners were listening to them. Suddenly there was such a violent earthquake that the foundations of the prison were shaken. At once all the prison doors flew open, and everyone's chains came loose. Acts 16:25-26^{NIV}

An open mouth can open doors. Can you recall the days when your praise was automatic? No matter how insignificant something seemed, you would emit instant praise. Well, it is time to get your praise back.

God does not crave your attention for His own gain. With or without you, He is untouchable, incomparable, and will always be superior. When He asks you to praise Him, He is requesting that you prioritize your praise and give Him permission to open and close doors on your behalf. Visualize this for a moment; your mouth is the barrel of a gun, and your praise is the bullet. If you load that barrel with the bullet and allow God to pull the trigger, you will be amazed at how quickly your atmosphere changes. Therefore, do not lose your praise. No! Not now. Let everything that has breath, praise the Lord. *Whoso offereth praise glorifieth me: and to him that ordereth his conversation aright will I shew the salvation of God. Psalm 50:23*

A woman once shared with me that she woke up one morning knowing there was no food in the house for her or her grandchild to eat. She said that as she stood at her window, pondering and staring into space, her eyes glanced at a fruit tree with only one fruit, a breadfruit. She picked the fruit, roasted it in a wood fire, and shared it with her grandchild. She further stated that she had no meat, so they ate it with butter. "Sis, while I was eating the breadfruit and butter, I felt so special. I took a praise break and started praising God for His power of provision. I couldn't believe that God placed one breadfruit on the tree at arm's length so we could have something to eat." Let everything that has breath, praise the Lord.

Beloved, given her situation, we would expect this woman to pity herself because of her lack. Instead, she chose to praise God for her gain. How about you? Do you still praise God despite your challenging circumstances, or do you pity yourself? Have you lost your praise? When did you lose it? Where did you abandon it? More importantly, how can you restore your praise? You cannot afford to lose your praise, for it will usher you through tough times. Your praise will give you peace even when others are suffering from depression. Your praise will bring you victory, while others are overcome by defeat; your praise will give you joy when others are sad; your praise can bring you freedom, while others are in bondage. You need your praise to disarm the enemy and to open doors that they have closed.

Beloved, be consistent with your praise. Praise God through your fears, praise through your tears, praise through your doubts, praise through your worries, and praise through your storms. When you praise in the midst of hardship, your situation will feel less cumbersome and more tolerable.

In Judges 1: 1-2, and Judges 20: 18, the Israelites inquired of the Lord, who should be sent into battle first, against the Canaanites, and the Benjaminites. He responded, "Send Judah first". Judah means praise. When you send up your praises before you enter into battle, you are giving God the permission to fight and defeat your enemies, on your behalf. When you lift your praises unto God, your children can be delivered from any addiction; you can be set free from the abusive relationship, and suicidal thoughts, frustration, and confusion, can be canceled and rendered powerless.

Command the spirit of praise to be restored in your life. Sometimes, you may not feel like praising or praying, but that is the time you should press beyond your feelings. Praising God does not depend on your feelings. How many times do you feel like not going to work but you went, anyway? You may say that you don't have the strength, but it's not by your might or by your power, but by the spirit of God which operates through you. When you are consistent with your praise, all limitations, previously placed on you, will be destroyed.

> Closed mouths close doors; but when you open your mouth to praise, doors will fling open.

Prayer

Dear Heavenly Father,

I will praise the marvelous works of Your hands. I bring praise on my lips and expectancy in my heart, and I will extol Your name, forever.

Jehovah Tehilati, God of praise, I confess that I have relinquished my praise to the enemy. O Mighty God, I ask that You restore unto me the spirit of praise, in Jesus' mighty name. Lord, I acknowledge that my praise has brought me through many sad and trying moments. It brought me deliverance and peace of mind. Father, I am aware that my praise gives You permission to fight for me, and overturn every guilty verdict handed down to me by the enemy. Restore my praise, O God, in Jesus' name.

Praise the Lord, O my soul and all that is within me, praise God. Jehovah Tehilati, God of my praise. The prayers and praises from Paul and Silas, flung prison doors open, saved the prison guard, and set them free. In the mighty name of Jesus, I command the nine systems of my body to praise You. In Jesus' mighty name, I command my bones, organs, and every member of my body to arise and praise You, the Creator. Father, In the mighty name of Jesus, may my praise break down prison bars, set captives free, and loose those who are bound. In the mighty name of Jesus, may my praise cause Satan' agents to turn against each other, cripple the works of the enemy, confuse their counsel, and destroy their plots.

In the mighty name of Jesus, I use the weapon of praise to pull down and destroy the stronghold of any evil conspiracy- the spirit of heaviness, and gloominess. In the name of Jesus, I use the weapon of praise to destroy all demonic sabotage, frustration, and confusion, in Jesus' name. Lord, with great expectation, I look forward to the restoration of my praise that will pull blessings towards me and defeat them that rise up against me. Adonai, restore unto me the kind of praise that will silence every tongue that speaks ill of me and confuse the agents and cohorts of Satan.

In the mighty name of Jesus, I refuse to be silenced anymore. In the name of Jesus, I will continuously sing praises unto the God of praise. Through the power in the blood of Jesus Christ, I rebuke every demon assigned to frustrate me and steal my praise. I command every assignment against my praise to be aborted right now, in the name of Jesus. In the name of Jesus, I reject the spirit of heaviness, and I put the garment of praise upon me. As of today, I will praise You continuously, for saving my soul and spearing my life.

Lord, I thank You for restoring my praise. Thank You for inhabiting my praise. Thank You for assigning angels to join me in praise. I love You, Lord. Blessed be the Lord, forevermore! In Jesus' name Amen. I will bless the Lord at all times: his praise shall continually be in my mouth. Psalm 34:1^{KJV}

Week 51 - Restore My Praise

Notes

Week 52

•••

RESTORE MY CONFIDENCE

So that we may boldly say, The Lord [is] my helper, and I will not fear what man shall do unto me. Hebrews 13:6^{KJV}

Though an host should encamp against me, my heart shall not fear: though war should rise against me, in this [will] I [be] confident. Psalm 27:3^{KJV}

Uncertainty has become a significant part of your life, which may have been precipitated by the words, "You will never amount to anything." Subconsciously, you carried those words, like pieces of luggage, throughout your life. You find it difficult to relate to anyone because your confidence has been replaced with feelings of inferiority, disbelief, and mistrust, which hinder your progress and sabotage your goals. You always doubt yourself and deem your life hopeless.

Beloved, replace those negative words with the Word of God. Repeat daily, the following: "I am fearfully and wonderfully made. I can do all things through Christ who gives me strength. I can do anything that I chose to do. I will accomplish my desired goals. I will no longer be enslaved by the negative words spoken over my life and planted in my spirit. I refuse to allow those words to interfere with who I am destined to become." Self-esteem is believing, with confidence, what God says about you and walking in that authority.

I encourage you to see yourself as a masterpiece in great demand. Hold your head high, and soar like an eagle. Rearrange your thoughts and recondition your mind while you restore your confidence. Believe that God has equipped you with the ability to do exceedingly well

Week 52 - Restore My Confidence

and to succeed. With that belief, you can restore your confidence and power to produce the life you've always wanted. Men may fail you, but you can rely on God. He is the ultimate esteem builder. *Have I not commanded you? Be strong and courageous. Do not be afraid; do not be discouraged, for the Lord your God will be with you wherever you go. Joshua 1:9^{NIV}*

Your abilities to do and to become far exceed your comprehension. Arise with self-assurance.

Prayer

Dear Heavenly Father,

I praise Your mighty name. Lord, You are magnificent. You are superb and excellent. I worship You for who You are. I give You praise, glory, and honor.

Jehovah Go'el, Lord my Redeemer, thank You for Your redemptive blood that was shed to set me free from all my sins. Father, please forgive me for all my iniquities, trespasses, and transgressions. Cleanse me from all unrighteousness. In the mighty name of Jesus, purge me from all impurities, and free my thoughts from negative thinking, in Jesus' mighty name.

Father, I confess that I lost confidence in myself and Your Word. I chose to accept the negative seeds that were planted and took root in my mind and heart. Adonai, hear me from Your sanctuary; and send help to free me from this bondage of low self-esteem and lack of confidence, in Jesus mighty name.

El Shaddai, the all-sufficient God, I ask that You restore my self-confidence and confidence in You, in Jesus' name. Lord, with unshakeable confidence and without fear, I declare that I am a masterpiece, in Jesus' name. I have the potential to be great and do exceptionally well, in Jesus' name. With confidence, I declare that I am in great demand because of my gifts and talents. I declare that I have the ability to do and become anything that I desire, in Jesus' name. I declare that I will no longer believe or give-in to the negative words hurled at me. In the name of Jesus, I refuse to let negative words dictate my performance, accomplishment, or overpower my existence.

Satan, with confidence I declare that the Lord is my light and my salvation. With boldness, I declare that I will not be afraid of what you or your cohorts will try to do to me, in Jesus' name. Though your host of demons and agents encamp against me, I will not fear. Though they may rage war against me I am confident that I will prevail because my God promised to fight my battles, hide me in His pavilion, and His secret place in the time of trouble, in Jesus' mighty name. Satan, with the restoration of my confidence, I will no longer believe Your lies about me. In the name of Jesus, I cancel every negative word spoken against me and my destiny. I decree and declare victory over every spirit of self-sabotage due to a lack of confidence, in Jesus' mighty name.

Elohim, thank You for the weapon of confidence to pull down and destroy the stronghold of low self-esteem, fear, and inferiority. Thank You for the assurance that my self-confidence has been restored. Thank You, Lord, for hearing and honoring my request to restore my confidence. Blessed be the Lord, forevermore! In Jesus' name Amen.

Week 52 - Restore My Confidence

Notes

A Call to Salvation

How is your relationship with God? Does your life feel fulfilled? Fulfillment is not determined by material wealth or your level of education. One can possess all of the aforementioned worldly abundance and still feel empty. Beloved, the only solution to fill that void within is to accept and acknowledge Jesus Christ as your Lord and Savior.

If you haven't seen it, you must have heard about the political instability, racial injustice, uncontrolled disease, along with other chaos and turmoil that's plaguing the land. Even though you are witnessing despicable and immoral behavior with your natural eyes, the world is experiencing a **spiritual attack** upon humankind. There is a battle underway in the spirit realm between God and Satan, for our souls. Don't be caught off guard.

Satan knows the King of Kings will return to Earth as a frowning judge to judge us according to our righteousness, and Satan will be sent to the pit of Hell, his final destination, once and for all. He understands this his reign on Earth is short, hence, he is working overtime to harvest as many souls as possible. Therefore, he influences the hearts of men to grow cold, and he tampers with emotions to prevent feelings of compassion, love, mercy, forgiveness, kindness, and fear of God. As a result, the Earth is experiencing an alarming rate of untimely deaths, immorality, men being lovers of themselves more than lovers of God, disrespect towards authority, and bloodshed. Panic and fear blanket the atmosphere, while many faces are veiled with uncertainty and unrest. Men are dying by the thousands, while many are wondering, "will I be next?" Many died without getting the chance to say, "Lord, have mercy". Many who did not seek salvation eventually died without the opportunity to repent of their sins and accept Jesus Christ as their Lord and Savior. Many will not experience eternal life with Christ; and death does not follow a schedule, so we never know when will be our last day.

A CALL TO SALVATION

Beloved, if you should die today, where would you spend eternity? If you are not born again, I encourage you to acknowledge Jesus Christ as the only way, the truth, and the life. Give Him your whole heart, today; surrender yourself to Him. You do not have to die without Christ. There is no repentance in the grave nor purgatory. Seek Him while He may be found; and call upon Him while He is near. Jesus endured excruciating pain and suffering so your soul would not be lost when you part this life. Don't allow His selfless sacrifice to have been in vain. Over the years, you may have heard that Jesus is coming soon, but you haven't seen Him yet. Don't get complacent and comfortable. If you take a closer look at the signs of the time you will be convinced that He is much closer than you think.

Whatever or whoever is holding you back from repenting and saying "Yes" to Jesus is not worth losing your life for. Let it or them go! Your soul is more valuable. I beseech you; say "Yes" to Jesus now! Tomorrow or next week is not promised to you, and it may be too late. Do not delay. Make God your priority, and everything else will fall into place.

As many as I love, I rebuke and chasten: be zealous therefore, and repent. [20]*Behold, I stand at the door, and knock: if any man hear my voice, and open the door, I will come in to him, and will sup with him, and he with me.* [22]*He that hath an ear, let him hear what the Spirit saith unto the churches. Revelation 3:19-20 & 22*[KJV]

Repentance Prayer

Dear Heavenly Father,

I humbly approach Your throne of mercy, admitting that I am a sinner. O, Mighty God, I acknowledge and declare that Jesus Christ is Lord. I surrender my heart, mind, body, and soul to You. Father God, I am willing and ready to accept Your invitation to salvation. I know You sent Your Son, Jesus Christ, to die for my sins so I could build a relationship with You and inherit eternal life.

Thank You, Father. Lord, in the mighty name of Jesus, I repent for harboring unforgiveness, bitterness, anger, iniquity, selfishness, pride, jealousy, envy, strife, malice, jealousy, covetousness, doubt, and unbelief, in my heart. Almighty God, cleanse my heart from all unrighteousness, and my mind from every evil thought, in Jesus' name. Father God, in the mighty name of Jesus, I ask that You purge and purify me with the precious blood of Your only begotten Son, Jesus Christ.

El Yeshuati, God of my salvation, thank You for hearing and answering my prayer. Thank You for washing and purging me with the blood of Jesus. Thank You for saving me so I can now declare that I am a new creation and a brand new man. In Jesus' mighty name, Amen.

Closing Prayer

A Prayer Just For You

Dear Heavenly Father,

Thank You for Your divine intervention in this project.

Father, I ask You for extraordinary blessings and uncommon favor upon all individuals who will read this Daily Restorational. Adonai, give a listening ear and a receptive heart to every reader while he or she reads this book, so they can hear Your voice and follow Your direction clearly, in Jesus' name.

Jehovah Jireh, my provider, You promised that You will supply all our needs. Father God, everything that this reader is in need of that is in Your perfect will, grant it unto him or her, right now. In the mighty name of Jesus, I decree and I declare that every reader's need is met, right now.

Jehovah Rophe, the Healer, In the mighty name of Jesus, I command all illnesses in this reader's body to be destroyed, by the consuming fire of God. Lord, You are touched by the feeling of their infirmities. Heal them, Lord, and they shall be healed. Save them and they shall be saved. In Jesus' name. God, You said in Your Word that healing is Your children's bread; and You have sent Your Word to heal. I am also reminded that by Your many stripes, we are healed. Father, in the name of Jesus, thank You healed the brokenhearted and bound up their wounds. Jehovah Rophe, thank You for being the Healer of all infirmities.

In the mighty name of Jesus, I bind cancer, diabetes, asthma, and rare blood diseases. In the mighty name of Jesus, I bind up eye problems, ears problems, thyroid problems, liver, lungs, heart and kidney diseases, autoimmune diseases, and all other ailments.

El Gibbor, in the name of Jesus, I come against and bind up the spirits of affliction and infirmities that are exalting themselves against this reader, right now. In the matchless name of Jesus, I rebuke every disease, bacteria, and viruses that may be lingering in your body right now.

Jehovah Rophe, in the name of Jesus, I command every bodily obstruction be removed. Lord, While You were here on earth You healed the sick, cleansed the lepers, raised the dead, and cast out devils; and You said greater things we shall do. Omnipotent Father, upon that reassurance, in the mighty name of Jesus, I command every and any abnormality in the body be healed, right now. With the power of the Almighty God vested in me, any other illness caused by demonic affliction, I strip you of your powers and assignment, and I render you powerless in Jesus' name. Through the authority in the blood of Jesus Christ, I command the spirit of infirmity to leave this body now and cast you out into outer darkness and dry places. Father, I replace every spirit of affliction and infirmity with the spirit of healing, joy, peace, deliverance, and Your blood.

Mighty God of Zion, through the power in the blood of Jesus, I speak to every financial drought in your life. There shall be no more lack, in Jesus' name. I call forth financial blessings from the East, West, North, and South. In the name of Jesus, I command all money that's been owed or promised to you, to be given to you, right now.

El Shaddai, every marriage that You ordained, in the name of Jesus, I command them to line up with Your promise that no man shall put them asunder. In the name of Jesus, I bind and rebuke any third party interference and the foul spirits that are trying to tear this marriage apart. In the name of Jesus, I speak love, respect, honor, and friendship in this marriage right now, through Jesus Christ, Your Lord.

Jehovah Mephalti, You are the one who delivers. I pray for the family of this reader, if there are children, I ask that You intervene with salvation, protection, and deliverance from the traps of the enemy.

Eloah, I ask that You release Your warrior angels to fight any agent of Satan who comes against them. Father, if there is a need that I fail to mention, fail not to grant it in Jesus' name. Jehovah Shalom, bring Your people perfect peace. Jehovah Tsori, God of Strength, strengthen those who are weak and draw closer to those who are sold out for You, in Jesus' name. Amen.

Appendix

Names of God – El

El - God (used 250 times)
El Echad - One God (Malachi 2:10)
El Hanne' eman - Faithful God (Deuteronomy 7:9)
El Emet - God of Truth (Psalm 31:5)
El Tsaddik - Righteous God (Isaiah 45:21)
El Shaddai - All-Sufficient God (Genesis 17:1; 28:3)
El Elyon - Most High God (Genesis 14:20; Psalm 9:2)
El Olam - Everlasting God (Genesis 21:33; Psalm 90:1-3)
El Ro'i - God Who Sees (me) (Genesis 16:13)
El Yeshurun - God of Jeshurun (Deuteronomy 32:15; Isaiah 44:2)
El Gibbor - Mighty God (Champion) (Isaiah 9:6)
El De' ot - God of Knowledge (1 Samuel 2:3)
El Haggadol - Great God (Deuteronomy 10:17)
El Hakkavod - God of Glory (Psalm 29:3)
El Hakkadosh - Holy God (Isaiah 5:16)
El Hashamayim - God of the Heavens (Psalm 136:26)
El Chaiyai - God of my Life (Psalm 42:8)
El-Channun - Gracious God (Jonah 4:2)
El Yisrael - God of Israel (Psalm 68:36)
El Sali - God of my Strength (Psalm 42:9)
El Erekh Apayim - God of Patience (Romans 15:5)
El Ha-tanchumim - God of Comfort (2 Corinthians 1:3-6)
El Rachum - God of Compassion (Deuteronomy 4:31)
El Yeshuatenu - God of our Deliverance (Psalm 68:19)
El-Kanno - Jealous God (Exodus 20:5)
El Hannora - Awesome God (Nehemiah 9:32)
El Kedem - Eternal God from Beginning (Deuteronomy 33:27)
El Mauzi - God of My Strength (Psalm 43:2)

El Mishpat - God of Justice (Isaiah 30:18)
El Selichot - God of Forgiveness (Nehemiah 9:17)
El Tehilati - God of My Praise (Psalm 109:1)
El Tzur – God, Our Rock (Deuteronomy 32:4)
El Yerush'lem - God of Jerusalem (2 Chronicles 32:19)
Immanuel - God with us (Isaiah 7:14)
Bethel (Beit-El) - House of El (Genesis 12:8)
Daniel - (Dani'el) My Judge Is Elohim (Ezekiel 14:14
Ezekiel (Yechezk' el) - God Strengthens (Ezekiel 1:3)
Gabriel (Gabri'el) - (Luke 1:19)
Israel (Yisrael) - God Contended For (Genesis 33:20)
Joel - YHWH Is God (Joel 1:1)
Michael (Mika'el) - Who Is Like God? (Jude 1:9)
Samuel (Shemu'el) - God Has Heard (Psalm 99:6)

Names of God – Jehovah

Jehovah – The Lord (Exodus 6:2-3)
Jehovah' Immeku – Lord is with You (Judges 6:12)
Jehovah' Ez Lami – Lord, My Strength (Psalm 28:7)
Jehovah' Izoz Hakaboth – Lord, Strong and Mighty (Psalm 24:8)
Jehovah' Ori – Lord, My Light (Psalm 27:1)
Jehovah' Uzam – Lord, Their Strength (Psalm 37:39)
Jehovah Adon Kal Ha'arets – Lord of All the Earth (Joshua 3:13)
Jehovah Adonai – Lord God (Genesis 15:2)
Jehovah Bara – Lord, Creator (Isaiah 40:28)
Jehovah Chatsahi – Lord, My Strength (Psalm 27:1)
Jehovah Chereb – The Lord, the Sword (Deuteronomy 33:29)
Jehovah Eli – Lord, My God (Psalm 18:2)
Jehovah Elyon – Lord, Most High (Psalm 38:2)
Jehovah Gador Milchamah – Lord, Mighty in Battle (Psalm 24:8)
Jehovah Ganan – Lord, Our Defense (Psalm 89:18)
Jehovah Go' el – Lord, Thy Redeemer (Isaiah 49:26; 60:16)
Jehovah Hashopet – Lord, the Judge (Judges 6:27)
Jehovah Hamelech – Lord, the King (Psalm 98:6)
Jehovah Helech' Olam – Lord, King Forever (Psalm 10:16)
Jehovah Melech' Olam – Lord, King Forever (Psalm 10:16)
Jehovah Hoshe' ah – Lord Save (Psalm 29:9)
Jehovah Jireh - Lord Will Provide (Genesis 22:14)
Jehovah Kabodhi – Lord, My Glory (Psalm 3:3)
Jehovah Kanna – Lord, Whose name is Jealous (Exodus 34:14)
Jehovah Keren Yish'i – Lord, Horn of my Salvation (Psalm 18:2)
Jehovah M'Kaddesh – Sanctifier (1 Corinthians 1:30)
Jehovah M'gaddishcem – Lord, Our Sanctifier (Exodus 31:13)
Jehovah Ma'oz – The Lord, My Fortress (Jeremiah 16:19)

Jehovah Machsi – Lord, My Refuge (Psalm 91:9)

Jehovah Magen – The Lord, the Shield (Deuteronomy 33:29)

Jehovah Mephalti – Lord, My Deliverer (Psalm 18:2)

Jehovah Metsodhathi – The Lord, My Fortress (Psalm 18:2)

Jehovah Misqabbi – Lord, My High Tower (Psalm 18:2)

Jehovah Naheh – Lord that Smites (Ezekiel 7:9)

Jehovah Nissi – Lord, Our Banner (Exodus 17:15; 1 Chronicles 29:11-13)

Jehovah Rophe – Lord that Heals (Exodus 15:26)

Jehovah Rohi – Lord, My Shepherd (Psalm 23:1)

Jehovah Sabaoth – Lord of Hosts (1 Samuel 1:3)

Jehovah Sel' i – Lord, My Rock (Psalm 18:2)

Jehovah Shalom – Lord, Our Peace (Judges 6:24)

Jehovah Shammah – Lord Is There (Ezekiel 48:35; Hebrews 13:5)

Jehovah Tsidkenu – Lord, Our Righteousness (Jeremiah 23:6; 1 Corinthians 1:30)

Jehovah Tsori – The Lord, My Strength (Psalm 19:14)

Jehovah Yasha – The Lord, Thy Savior (Isaiah 49:26; 60:16)

Note of Thanks

Hip, hip, hooray! The long-awaited "Daily Restorational" is here. I am humbled by the many words of encouragement and support I've received from family, friends, and readers of my books. Words cannot express my gratitude and appreciation to you for believing in my God-given assignments, for seeing my potential, and for motivating me, as I model the excellence of Christ. Thank you for helping to propel the ministries which God entrusted in my care. I appreciate your many prayers. It is a blessing to have you in my corner, aiding in the evangelizing of God's words of encouragement to our brothers and sisters. Moreover, thank you for the opportunity to minister to your spirit-man, your mind, your flesh, and your emotions. I enjoy engaging with you.

May the joy of the Lord continue to be your strength; and may the love of God keep your mind in perfect peace.

Peace be unto you all.
Evangelist Jasmine Gordon
Servant of God

References

Dictionary: Merriam-Webster
Bible: Old & New Testament
KJV, NIV, AMPLIFIED

About the Author

Jasmine was born as Nichole Gordon on the island of Jamaica. She is the eighth of nine children. Her talents span many fields. She is the founder of Ministries Without Boundaries International, a non-profit organization that caters to the material needs of others. Since 2011, she has hosted an annual banquet and concert on both Mother's Day and Father's Day, which brings smiles to the families in her community. As an Evangelist and a Chaplain, Jasmine strongly believes that, once someone's earthly needs are met, they will be more inclined to hear God's messages of love and hope.

Despite maintaining such a busy schedule, Jasmine finds time to engage in her "secular ministries," which include nursing, coaching, consulting, and developing online courses. She is also a radio personality, the CEO and owner of a very successful assisted living facility, and the author of three published books, titled: *Fear Not! There is Still Power in Prayer* and *38 Reasons for Unanswered Prayers* and *Daily Restorational-52 Weeks of Devotion*.

Moreover, Jasmine is an entrepreneur who empowers and coaches individuals in the health field as well as everyday men and women who are hungry for change and wish to maximize their full potential. Using her online courses, workshops, conferences, seminars, and retreats, she guides and supports clients across the world.

Jasmine is also the proud mother of a 32-year-old son and grandmother of a 4-year-old grandson. She presently resides in Palm

Bay, Florida, where she often plans and coordinates uplifting events for the community. Jasmine makes a habit of guiding, encouraging, and empowering others. She strives to see the potential for greatness in other people and illuminates their capabilities. Jasmine feels most content when those around her are transformed and lead fulfilling lives.

Those who know Jasmine and have been influenced by her presence or her ministries understand the philanthropic impact she can have in her community. Jasmine is a trailblazer and woman of profound strength and resilience. What will she do next?

www.ingramcontent.com/pod-product-compliance
Lightning Source LLC
Chambersburg PA
CBHW071224080526
44587CB00013BA/1490